SNAPSHOTS *of* *Hope* & HEART

A **WORD** *Girls* Collective

Snapshots of Hope & Heart
©2021 by Kathy Carlton Willis
www.kathycarltonwillis.com

ISBN-13: 978-1-7330728-5-4

Published by 3G Books, Beaumont, TX 77706

www.threegbooks.com

Copyedited by Kathy Carlton Willis

Editing, Interior, and Cover Design by Michelle Rayburn
www.missionandmedia.com

A WORD*Girls* Collective

Foreword by WordGirls Founder, Kathy Carlton Willis

SNAPSHOTS *of*
Hope & HEART

A 12-Week Devotional to
Shine the Light on God's Word

3G BOOKS

Contents

HOPE

HEART

A Foreword by Our Founder

Snapshots capture memories to be shared with others. In this WordGirls collective, we researched what God's Word says about the topics of *hope* and *heart*. The authors inserted stories, much like snapshots, to help us capture a true-to-life inspirational insight fitting for the daily Scripture. We hope the takeaways will stick with you throughout the day, similar to the memory of a snapshot long after you've tucked it away.

We wish for you:

- A slice of life captured in full color to treasure forever. (Lisa-Anne Wooldridge)
- Quick, heartwarming shots that will keep something or someone close to your heart. (Mindy Cantrell)
- An opportunity to consider what you've learned, what you've lost, and what you've gained from the experience captured by the "camera." (Denise Margaret Ackerman)

Our prayer is that these words will deliver word pictures of hope and heart to save to your mind's photo album. In that frame of reference, the Bible is the faith family album deserving to be passed down through the generations.

When we hear the word *snapshot*, we think moments.

- A suspended moment in time—a precious memory of something dear to your heart that you want to have with you forever. (Nancy Graves)

- Little moments in our lives that are frozen in our mind's eye—moments that mean something to our hearts. (Betty Predmore)
- Small but significant moments that stick with you over time. Moments you look back on with emotion—good, bad, or otherwise—and realize they changed you in some way and made you into the person you are today. (Teresa Janzen)
- Unstaged or surprise still shots—not necessarily when I was at my best, but when it was more important to capture the moment than perfection. (Gina Stinson)
- A God adventure in everyday life. A vignette, or glimpse, of God's involvement in that moment captured in our memories. We can reflect back on these when we encounter a similar situation. (Charlaine Martin)
- The top ten snapshots in my life. Those moments I recall so clearly—as if I had a photograph of the scene—that were impactful. Not always good, but pivotal in some way. (Hally Wells)

Take your own snapshots as you look through our album of hope and heart.

Your WordGirlfriend,

Kathy Carlton Willis, WordGirls Founder
God's Grin Gal

About WordGirls

In 1994 I had a brainchild to start a group to coach fun, faith-filled women who were serious about the writing life. I served on faculty at national writer's conferences and realized attendees remained stuck in the writing process. I'd see them come back year after year with their projects showing little progress. They were often overwhelmed by the conference material and didn't know how to apply it to their writing lives. They needed a group to keep them accountable and a coach to help them figure out their next steps.

I'm grateful to Deb DeArmond, who worked tirelessly with me through the launch process of this wonderful group of women. Her assistance and brainstorming helped me birth my vision for the group.

WordGirls is a special sisterhood of writing support for women who write from a biblical worldview (whether for the faith market or general market). We propel writers to the next level—regardless of where they are today.

Here's an overview of our exclusive WordGirls benefits:

1. Once-per-year, one-hour phone coaching to personalize your advancement as a writer and/or speaker.

2. Private Facebook group to interact, brainstorm, pray for each other, share ideas, ask questions, etc.

3. Monthly topics to help you grow as a writer. To enhance your learning, the topics will be covered through Facebook group discussions and Zoom live sessions (recorded for you to watch later if you can't make it live).

4. Downloadable PDFs offer extra training in the form of tutorials.

5. Weekly study hall. We designate a two-hour period to work on projects we call our B.I.C. time (butt in chair). Study hall provides added accountability.

6. Periodic challenges. Some challenges are month-long, and others last a season. These challenges will stretch you without overwhelming you. Guaranteed to increase productivity if you participate. (Participation is not required to be a member.)

7. Digital membership badge to post on your website or social media page.

8. Reduced rates for events and for-fee materials. We have online retreats and WordGirls@Home intensives. When safe to meet in person, we will also offer WordGirls Getaways again.

9. Opportunity to submit writing for our WordGirls publications.

10. Additional services when you hire our coach for a reduced hourly rate.

If you have questions, email kathy@kathycarltonwillis.com. To keep the group intimate, a limited number of memberships are granted. We only have open enrollment twice per year: in January (for a February to January membership period) and in July (for an August to July membership period). The registration form can be found at kathycarltonwillis.com/wordgirls.

We also open up the online and in-person retreats to non-members, so keep an eye on the website for details of upcoming events.

Hope

Signs and Wonderfuls

by Lisa-Anne Wooldridge

I pray that God, the source of hope, will fill you completely with joy and peace because you trust in him. Then you will overflow with confident hope through the power of the Holy Spirit.

ROMANS 15:13 (NLT)

MY LITTLE SISTER took the blackberries from my hand and looked at me in awe. We were in the woods where I was feeding her lunch, picked straight from the earth around us. I pulled up cattail stalks and gave her the clean, tender edible part. Some wild garlic gave us greens, but she puckered her lips at the bitter flavor. It was a beautiful day for an adventure. Responsibility for her wellbeing was up to me as the ten-year-old big sister.

Glorious blue skies with fluffy cotton ball clouds played backdrop to chatty birds and swooping butterflies. Maple trees grew in a circle, giving us sanctuary from the wild tom turkeys. I weaved everything into the story—the tall grass was a hiding place for fairies and little-enough girls, the upturned tree with gnarly roots homed a gnome, and the shallow pond sheltered enchanted frogs who sang for their supper. The winds in the redbud trees were invisible angels, watching over us, laughing at our silly faces. Dragonflies were her favorite. Jewel-toned with diamond wings—tiny queens and kings.

Wonderfuls, she called my stories. "Tell me more wonderfuls." Her words came to my memory as I stood, for the first time in many years, in the spot where we had played as little girls. Sobs shook my whole body, the woods were gone, and only a barren field remained with a few scraggly maple trees. My sister was gone too.

I'd come to this place right after her funeral, hoping to find some trace of her here. Knees weak, heart broken, and hope evaporating. Could I really trust God with one of my most precious people? Was she safe in his arms? Was he taking over the job of telling her all the wonderfuls now?

I looked down at the base of a tree and found a small patch of blackberries growing rich and ripe, a month early for their season. I plucked a handful, holding them out for my sister, and then savored each sweet and precious bite. A dragonfly landed on a branch nearby, and a breeze stirred the trees.

I understood the message. Keep hope. Receive peace. Go out with joy. The *wonderfuls* are new every morning.

Father, thank you that we are not a people without hope! Fill me to overflowing with joy and peace in believing. Open my eyes to see all the wonders you've created for me as I trust in you. Thank you for keeping safe everything I give into your care and for leading me by your Spirit all the way safely home.

Cleaning House

by Teresa Janzen

*Let your unfailing love surround us, LORD, for
our hope is in you alone.*

PSALM 33:22 (NLT)

O N MY WEDDING day, I became an instant mother to three young children—one with special needs. Within three years, we had added two more to our brood. Life became a never-ending cycle of laundry, spilled Cheerios, and scraped knees.

One Sunday morning during my women's small group, I broke down in tears. "I just don't know how to manage. There's not a clean dish in the cupboard nor an inch of visible carpet in the living room."

That afternoon, three of the ladies from my small group—brooms and buckets in hand—showed up at my front door. Every aspect of my messy house was instantly exposed. One woman washed dishes, another moved from room to room with a trash bag. The third removed the crying baby from my arms and pressed a cup of tea into my hand.

While God's unfailing love surrounds us always, it is never more apparent than in our most despairing moments. When we throw up our hands and cry out to him, he swoops in to clean house. But we must be willing to open the door. He wants to look in every room—even under the sofa cushions and behind the furniture. As we are willing to allow access, God will clear out the rubbish and make a suitable dwelling for us to live together in relationship with him.

Cleaning house is not something we can do on our own. We quickly find ourselves in such dishevelment that we don't know where to begin to tackle the problem. Assurance of God's unfailing love brings hope as we begin the process of exposing and clearing the mess: poor self-image, bad attitudes, bitterness, apathy, doubt, fear, confusion, etc. When the work begins, it may be uncomfortable. Before long, we see progress, encouraging us to give access to even more rooms.

> My loving God, I can't tackle this mess on my own. I invite you in and give you full access. Help me see the cause of chaos and identify a way forward. I surrender to you and ask that you help me clear away all that is hindering me from enjoying your presence. Thank you for the hope found in your unfailing love.

I'm Gonna Let It Shine!

by Beth Kirkpatrick

O, LORD, you alone are my hope. I've trusted you, O LORD, from childhood.

PSALM 71:5 (NLT)

HAT COULD BE better than splashing in a pool on a hot summer day? When I was a kid, we always looked forward to getting together with our cousins at Grandma's country home on the Fourth of July. The afternoon began with lots of swimming. Then whoever was handy helped shuck sweet corn, and Grandpa barbecued steaks and burgers. After a dish of homemade vanilla ice cream, we had to wait a whole hour before we could hop back into the water.

When it finally got dark, we threw some clothes over our still-damp swimsuits and impatiently waited with chlorine-reddened eyes for the fireworks to begin. Our dads were in charge of the big fireworks, but we kids got to frolic with the sparklers. I loved it when my sparkler was lit first. My light sizzled and threw off tiny sparks. Then my light touched the tip of someone else's, and there would be a bright little explosion. The two of us jumped and skipped and drew and wrote with the fiery ends in the air. When I saw my sparkler fading, I shook the box for more. Nothing was sadder than the realization that all the sparklers were gone, and we would have to wait another year to enjoy them again.

God has given us the spectacular task of sharing the story of his love and mercy with everyone we meet. As we share with others, the Holy Spirit lights the flame of faith, spreading the joy of knowing the Lord from person to person. But unlike my little cardboard container of sparklers with its finite number of pieces, God provides us with a limitless supply of his power and love.

We need never fear that his care for us will sputter out and disappear into the darkness. And remember, even though our Dad is in charge of the big fireworks, he has given us the responsibility and joy of dancing with the sparklers. God is working in you and through you to achieve his purposes. Sparkle in the darkness with God's hope and love!

Lord, kindle my flame of faith and help me to share it joyfully. Help me to remember that your love and mercy are infinite and more than enough to brighten the darkness of our world. You alone are my hope.

Hope-in-Heart Surgery

by Nancy Graves

*When doubts filled my mind, your comfort gave
me renewed hope and cheer.*

PSALM 94:19 (NLT)

I WAS BORN WITH a hole in my heart. It was 1963, and the field of pediatric cardiology was considered pioneer territory. At the time, surgery on infants with congenital heart defects was seen as risky and controversial. My mother told me later that people with my condition, left untreated, became invalids by age twenty and didn't live long into adulthood. The stressful reality and physical strain of life would be too much for me. I needed open-heart surgery.

It was a dire situation, but I had Dr. Miller. In his expert opinion, it was best to wait until I grew enough to gain a better prognosis. He would monitor me, watching closely over my condition until just the right time. The benefits outweighed the risks.

As I grew, so did the hole in my heart. Being a child, I didn't understand the gravity of the situation. Though the threat to my life increased daily, I just wanted to run and play like the other kids. Only, I couldn't keep up. *What if I never could? Would life always be this hard?* I began to worry.

But one thing I knew for sure—I loved Dr. Miller. He was kind and always greeted me with a smile. His soft-spoken manner was calming, his hand on my shoulder, a comfort. Any fear I had was put to rest, and my outlook brightened immediately.

At age seven, just a wisp of a girl, I was finally ready for my operation. Dr. Miller was careful and gentle, which helped me hope to have a future. Thanks to his keen supervision, timing, and skill, I'm still here today. A testament to his excellent work.

Is the stress and strain of life too much sometimes? Are you winded from trying to keep up and worried you never will? Maybe it's a dire situation, but you have God!

Like Dr. Miller, God, in his *perfect* direction and timing, allows what seems to hold us back and weigh us down. He rarely steps in right away to remove our problems. Instead, knowing the benefit of spiritual growth that outweighs the risk of our premature development, he waits and watches. Then, at just the right time and with surgical precision, he steps in to do what he does best: hope-in-heart surgery.

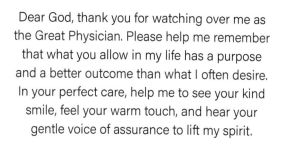

Dear God, thank you for watching over me as the Great Physician. Please help me remember that what you allow in my life has a purpose and a better outcome than what I often desire. In your perfect care, help me to see your kind smile, feel your warm touch, and hear your gentle voice of assurance to lift my spirit.

I Can't, but He Can!

by Charlaine Martin

To them God chose to make known how great among the Gentiles are the riches of the glory of this mystery, which is Christ in you, the hope of glory.

COLOSSIANS 1:27 (ESV)

*G*OD DID IT again. He sustained Don's strength. I listened, watchful as my husband preached boldly from 1 Peter 1:17–21. The authority of God's message shone in his posture as a baby's coos from the crowd sang back-up to his unshakable voice. "If we don't have that relationship with God through the cleansing of his Son's blood—and the faith that comes from it—all is lost. But when we have that firm foundation in the kingdom of God, we let go of this place as our temporary home."

While a soft hymn played, Don offered the opportunity for anyone to accept Jesus as Savior. Some came for prayer, while others asked about salvation. With compassion, he knelt to pray with each one. When he finished, he led the congregational prayer, then dismissed us with a blessing.

People rose from their seats, chatting on the way out. Their pastor's cancer-weary body, zapped of energy, leaned against the podium. I walked with Don as he shuffled home for a nap. End-stage cancer and its treatments hit him hard.

Other patients discussed deep faith issues with him during chemotherapy. He listened and prayed with those who received devastating news. Some church members drew inspiration from him despite their challenges. Empowered, they sought opportunities to share Jesus with their neighbors.

Don said he felt humbled. As he relayed stories to me, we were awestruck by how God worked in him, through him, and to him. He marveled as a single mom generously shared her meager resources with neighbors. He found hope from a woman undergoing intense radiation treatments. Frequently, he drew strength from people God entrusted to his care. It's a comfort to know that now, in eternity, Don can effortlessly sing praises before God. As I consider his sacrifices, I'm inspired to keep writing about God-adventures when illness zaps my energy.

Paul wrote to the Colossian church while under house arrest, plagued by his own limitations. He encouraged them to continue teaching the truth even when they faced strong arguments against his teachings: "That's why I work and struggle so hard, depending on Christ's mighty power that works within me" (Colossians 1:29 NLT). Paul struggled, but God strengthened him to continue his ministry. His example encouraged the early churches.

We all have a ministry. God strengthens us to share his gift of salvation despite our struggles and limitations. Who inspires you to tell others about God's love? Be encouraged by their example. No matter what you face, rely on God's strength to offer others hope.

Lord, I don't have the strength to do what you've called me to do. You've given me faithful examples to show me how to share Jesus with people, but I am weak. Please, help me. I need your strength to share hope and how you've changed my life. I'm honored you chose me to be your messenger of hope.

Land Ho on Love's Shore!

by Becki James

Love never gives up, never loses faith, is always
hopeful, and endures through every circumstance.

1 CORINTHIANS 13:7 (NLT)

*T*ODAY, I AM celebrating! With a tiramisu double-scoop in one hand and a writing pad snugged under the steering wheel, I am parked on a slope overlooking the lake. Long and narrow, this shoreline is sprinkled with places to pull over for ice cream bliss. While keeping the creamy drips at bay, I hear the muffled shouts of the yacht instructor preening his fleet into an obedient line. The last white sail bobs into position before nearby gulls shriek on the dock, bickering over abandoned crumbs. I smile at a lady passing by with her dog, who apparently thinks chasing birds is standard procedure on bay watch.

This exact spot and I go way back. Captured in unwritten memoirs, it holds a history of my faith. You see, this is where I used to come to cry. My saddest conversations churned on this bank. Not really a celebration oasis, right? But it is.

If life had a ship's log, mine would tell tales of a "lifeboat" lost at sea and springing leaks. Despite navigational planning, my family drifted off course. Circumstances overpowered me. I was drowning at the helm. As mercy had it, I stole away here, sails tattered, docked in my beat-up minivan. With white crests beating against the jetty, I cast questions to heaven. Summer. Winter. Spring. Fall. I think my uncertainties outlived several vehicles. Yet, the waves remained a steady lull for my soul.

Hope is like that. Like the ebb and flow of the sea breaking upon the shore, hope regenerates from the depths of God's character. Because his love never fails, we have the courage to withstand life's storms. Turmoil may surge over us—plunging us beneath the surf. But hope drags fear back to the enemy's deep trenches, resurfacing as a cool zephyr of God's presence across our face.

Even when adrift in the dismal heat of discouragement, hope lifts stagnant air, revealing the glassy reflection of God's power. Because of who God is, we have a limitless source of love.

Here in this spot, I found sustaining hope. God used the vessel of my rickety van to lead me to the shores of his character. As faithful as the tides, God's love is everlasting. Today I am celebrating that I no longer need to abandon hope, resigning myself to prevailing winds, because I will never sail beyond the coordinates of his love.

> Abba Father, thank you that your love never gives up on me. Thank you for showing me that my hope rests in your love for me. Help me to look to your character when storms arise and know the power of your unfailing love.

Sober Rest

by Kelly Herr

But since we belong to the day, let us be sober,
having put on the breastplate of faith and love,
and for a helmet, the hope of salvation.

1 Thessalonians 5:8 (esv)

S HE TOLD ME to rest and left me alone. What hard advice to follow! I could a thousand times more easily have read another book or attended a class.

As a child, I dealt with trauma and learned to cope. Mom's schizophrenia and sexual abuse were two reasons I became a day-dreamer and found solace on a tennis court. Although I became a Christian as a young child, my poor choices as a young adult led to consequences that held me in a very dark place with no hope for healing. I turned to God again and committed to living my life for him—to please him. Foolishly, I strived to please everyone, and I did everything I could to make others happy. My life mission was to outrun my past, and I ran for thirty years.

I finally talked with a counselor, admitting I was exhausted and stuck. We discussed my childhood and my regrets. She told me that as a Christian, I was forgiven, complete, healed, and free. She explained the price for my sins was paid by Jesus on the cross, and I didn't need to work for salvation or acceptance. I didn't believe her. It was too easy. As I left, I asked her about homework. I couldn't wait for the next assignment to improve myself. Instead, she told me to rest.

Watching Mom rest embodies my memories of childhood. She was either in bed or in a mental hospital. I never rested because rest was painful. But as I made myself sit quietly, I experienced God's peace. I allowed myself to feel the pain of my past, and I began to cry—something else I never allowed myself to do. But this cry was cleansing and healing. It felt good. I realized I had numbed my pain by working hard and doing good deeds, but it wasn't effective at addressing my issues. Like alcohol, it was temporary and did not satisfy for very long.

By leaning into the pain, I allowed myself to feel. At first, it was difficult, but then it was peaceful. This was resting. I began to live life restored and renewed.

As Christians, we're called to be sober, not intoxicated by the world's standards. Today, my sobriety means that I rest in Jesus, putting my hope and faith in him, loving him above all else. One day at a time.

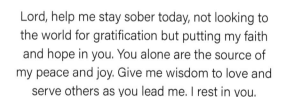

Lord, help me stay sober today, not looking to the world for gratification but putting my faith and hope in you. You alone are the source of my peace and joy. Give me wisdom to love and serve others as you lead me. I rest in you.

SNAPSHOTS OF HOPE & HEART

My Heart Tuned to His Glory

by Joanie Shawhan

We look forward with hope to that wonderful
day when the glory of our great God and Savior,
Jesus Christ, will be revealed.

TITUS 2:13 (NLT)

I WONDER IF MY heart will burst with joy on that wonderful day when I see Jesus face-to-face in the fullness of his glory. I can't wait to worship him there.

Until then, I think God gives me snapshots of hope when he breaks through my mundane tasks with his glorious presence. How I cherish those occasions when I sense his comfort and peace through Scripture, worship, and prayer. I call these times *glory moments.*

For example, one day during a church service, I listened to a familiar passage of Scripture. The words "I am not angry with you" reverberated in my ears. I had never read that translation before, but God made sure I heard those exact words. The truth of God's Word broke a lie I believed. God was not angry with me—a glory moment.

Another time, I wasn't sure I would survive the loss of a loved one. Tears streamed down my cheeks as I listened to the words of a worship song. Through those lyrics, God assured me I would be okay—a glory moment.

I'm reminded of when I had injured my back and was unable to work. I stood on a knoll overlooking a park and asked God to heal my back. I wondered if he would answer my prayer.

While walking home, I noticed the stiffness in my spine had disappeared. I stopped, not sure if I imagined the eased tension. I gently rotated my spine to the right, then to the left. No pain! Jesus had answered my prayer and healed my back—a glory moment.

I treasure those times when I experience the presence of the Lord, whether my eyes well with tears during worship, a Scripture touches my heart, or God answers prayer. Maybe these moments are a foretaste of that wonderful day when Jesus will be fully revealed.

Until that day, I'll tune my heart to listen for his voice—the glory moments.

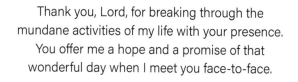

Thank you, Lord, for breaking through the mundane activities of my life with your presence. You offer me a hope and a promise of that wonderful day when I meet you face-to-face.

Blind Faith

by Betty Predmore

Let us hold tightly without wavering to the hope we affirm, for God can be trusted to keep his promise.

HEBREWS 10:23 (NLT)

OTHERHOOD IS SUCH a blessing, but it can also cause us to feel significant times of helplessness. Despite those moments when we can't fix everything for our children, there are also little tidbits of time that are so sweet they bring us to tears. I had the joy of experiencing one such occasion recently with my eldest daughter.

We were at another appointment with the eye specialist. My daughter's vision had diminished so much, she was lucky to read the top letter in the eye chart.

But this visit held hope. A contact in the eye was supposed to restore some of the lost vision brought on by Graves' disease. We were there so she could get fitted for the contact that would go in the right eye and get the cornea transplant scheduled for the left eye.

The doctors did many tests that day. Then a specialist came in, put some drops in my girl's eye, and inserted a contact. Another check of the eye chart, and she got all the way to 20/50. She asked my daughter to wait in the waiting area for about fifteen minutes to let the contact settle in.

I followed her and sat down beside her.

I saw her dabbing at her eyes, even the one that hadn't been touched. Concerned, I asked her if the other eye was irritated. She turned toward me, and I saw tears streaming down her cheeks. "No, mom," she answered. "I'm just crying because I can see your face."

My heart broke for this sweet child who has been missing so much. My heart rejoiced that she could make out my face. And my hope soared that finally, this beloved daughter of mine would have her vision restored.

I held her in my embrace as her tears flowed, and I thanked God for walking alongside my daughter throughout this ordeal. He promises to never leave us. He walks through our fires with us. Sometimes ahead of us, forging our trail, and sometimes beside us, carrying us when we cannot stand.

I have spent many hours in hospitals and doctors' offices. There are times I've felt exasperated, frustrated, and downright mad. None of that compares to the simple, pure, and beautiful joy of those precious moments that are gifts from our Father. Those struggles don't hold a candle to a child's happy tears of hope and excitement.

Father, thank you that you are always there. I thank you for choosing the unexpected moments to bless my socks off and for providing healing, especially when I feel hopeless. I'm so grateful you are a constant source of hope. When we cannot see, you give us faith—you give me faith. May I use it to help others see you.

Godly Lightbulb Moments

by Terri Kirby

*Lead me by your truth and teach me, for
you are the God who saves me. All day long
I put my hope in you.*

PSALM 25:5 (NLT)

*A*ND THE EASTER Bunny?" Heart-breaking gasp. "And SANTA CLAUS?" I saw the imaginary lightbulb over my young daughter's head and the mixed emotions on her face. She had realized first that I was the tooth fairy and then that obviously I must also be the Easter Bunny and Santa Claus.

I thought I was quite sneaky at the other roles, but I knew I had stunk as tooth fairy. Whoever came up with the idea to sneak into a child's bedroom and grab an old tooth under their sleeping head truly enjoyed a challenge.

My daughter's revelation reminds me how God reveals his truth to us bit by bit as we are ready to comprehend it. He knows our hearts and shares his wisdom with us in small pieces at a time as we are able to grasp it. I get chills knowing that the Creator of the universe, who is all-knowing, all-powerful, and present everywhere, cares so much about little old me. He works with the strengths he's given me and looks past my weaknesses.

I can have hope that even when I feel I've disappointed him, he knows my heart. Each day, he will give me what I need to become more of the person he wants me to become.

When we commit our lives to Christ, our sins are forgiven. Yet, we still sin. As long as we sincerely repent, he will continue to forgive us. God looks at the heart, not merely the outward actions because he knows we are still sinners. He considers our motives, which are the reasons why we do or don't do something. Even "religious" and "Christian" actions can be performed for the wrong reasons and with improper motives. God sees and knows all.

I rest in his love, assured in the fact that he sees my heart—the heart of a saved sinner who each day wants to please him—and he's drawing me deeper into his will for my life. Even when I am going through a hard time, I can find hope and strength because he knows my heart and will enlighten and guide me step by step, day by day. Praise God!

Dear Lord, thank you that you care so deeply about me that you see beyond my weaknesses and into my heart. I praise you for revealing new truths to me about yourself, myself, others, and your world. Thank you for considering the level I am at in my walk with you and building on my growth bit by bit as I can digest.

Hold On Tight

by Mindy Cantrell

*Through Christ you have come to trust in God. And
you have placed your faith and hope in God because he
raised Christ from the dead and gave him great glory.*

1 PETER 1:21 (NLT)

*H*OLD ON, MINDY, just hold on," my good friend Cheryl
said to me.

With frustrated tears stinging my weary eyes, I retorted,
"Ugh! If I hear that phrase one more time, I'm going to scream!
Hold on to what?" My car was broken down, and I had no way to
get to work. My young daughter was sick, and I had no way to get
her to the doctor. There was no one to care for Tiffany while she
was sick and no money left to pay for any of it.

Looking back at that difficult time, I can see God's hand at
work. I sure couldn't then. The great wall of trials in my life had
separated me from the shaky trust I thought I had in God's plan.
But, oh dear reader, God did have a plan.

In my despair that day, Cheryl asked God to show up in a
mighty way. And show up he did. First, Cheryl drove us to urgent
care, where I was allowed to charge the bill. Next, after speaking

with my mom, it turned out she'd kept her old car when she up-graded, and she *gave* me the old one. And then, unbelievably, I was able to sell my broken car back to the used car dealer for what I owed on it. With no upcoming car payment, I could pay Tiffany's medical bills. God proved faithful.

When we seek God with all our hearts, we will find him, and he will help us. After I quieted my struggling and reached for him, he was there. He soothed my anxiety and replaced my debt with hope and a better way for my future. Through this experience, God drew me closer and transformed my shaky trust into firm faith.

Our God, from the very beginning, proved his love and provided hope for us by the promise of Jesus's resurrection from the empty tomb. And through Jesus, he raises us up from broken dreams and empty faith and allows us to cling to him as he bathes us with hope and peace. All we must do is seek him with all our hearts and hold on tight while he works things out for good. Will you quiet your struggle and seek God today?

Dear God, thank you for your faithful promises that soothe my anxiety and give me hope. When I am weak and overwhelmed, please draw me close and help me hold tightly to you. Fill me with your peace as I trust that you have a plan and will work it out for me. Please help my faith and hope in you grow strong and sure.

This Is Taking Too Long

by Sandy Lipsky

*I am worn out waiting for your rescue, but I
have put my hope in your word.*

PSALM 119:81 (NLT)

I HATE TO WAIT. I wanted a baby. Married for over three years, my husband and I felt ready to add to our family. Little did I know the wait we had in store.

My sister and I married brothers. Our weddings were three years apart. When they faced infertility, they suggested we also see a specialist. Upset by their news and the suggestion, I told myself we would be fine. It was their problem not ours.

After a few years with no success, we saw a specialist. The temperature charts began. Depression and exhaustion followed. We tried surgeries. Nothing helped.

"How long, Lord?" I cried. No answer.

Well-meaning people shared story after story of friends and family who became pregnant once they "relaxed." I AM RELAXED! Deep down, however, in the place no one sees, I whispered, "What if that doesn't happen for me? What if our infertility never goes away?"

Someone from our church in Michigan knew of our struggles and gave me a book that had helped her. I wish I could remember the title. The author shared her struggles with infertility. Despite her pain, God brought her to a place of acceptance. She experienced peace and joy in childlessness. After reading how the author yielded to God's plan, I bowed my head and cried.

In an act of submission, I laid my dream of motherhood at the Savior's feet. If his plan for our family did not include children, I would still hope in the Lord. When I made the decision to accept childlessness, a peace that surpasses understanding flooded my heart.

A few months later, I felt a strong urge to call a local adoption agency. Both my husband and I agreed to pursue this hope. My sister and brother-in-law had adopted a little girl a few years prior and laid the groundwork for us. Almost one year exactly from the day I contacted the agency, we held the most beautiful baby girl in our arms.

Worn out from waiting, I had laid my dreams at the feet of my Father. He picked them up, wiped away my sorrow, and in his loving-kindness turned my hope into joy.

Your plans for me are better than any I can come up with. Even when I don't understand what you are doing, I will trust you. Thank you for rescuing my dreams and giving me hope in the wait.

Winning Hope

by Gina Stinson

*Hope deferred makes the heart sick, but
a dream fulfilled is a tree of life.*

PROVERBS 13:12 (NLT)

*D*EFLATED SPIRITS HUDDLED together in the dugout. The game had not gone as planned. As the team geared up for their last inning, they knew their final chance at bat would result in a loss unless a miracle happened. Within moments, what they had worked for, planned for, and anticipated would be a memory. But in classic movie fashion, the underdog snagged a win at the last minute. Fans cheered, spirits soared, and celebration ignited. In the span of mere seconds, withered hope transformed into winning hope.

Truth be told, we've all experienced discouragement in some area of our lives. Hopelessness leaves us feeling knocked down, depressed, and without purpose. It makes us heartsick. The loss of a job, the perils of parenting, the heartache of divorce, the burden of financial woes—all can leave us wondering if our hard work and effort are really worth it. When our eyes are on our circumstances, emptiness and despair feel close.

But for those of us who know Christ, confident hope is available. And hope brings life. Hope reminds us this is not the end. Rise or fall, success or defeat, healing or death—there is life beyond the spinning of this earth. There is life eternal!

When God turns our situations around, it brings hope. When he provides healing or restores a relationship, life is breathed back into our weakened lungs. Let's not forget—God changes hopeless situations. Jesus gave us eternal life and eternal hope when he died on the cross for us.

Whether or not God heals, fixes, mends, or changes our problems and challenges here on earth, we can be filled with life-giving hope because we know who holds eternity in his hands. True, lasting hope is only found in him. We win with him.

Lord, thank you for the hope you give us. Forgive me when my eyes focus on the hardships and struggles of this life. Remind me of the eternal hope I have, even when things don't go as I plan here on earth. Thank you for the eternal hope found in Jesus.

Fit for a King

by Lisa-Anne Wooldridge

*As for the rich in this present age, charge them
not to be haughty, nor to set their hopes on the
uncertainty of riches, but on God, who richly
provides us with everything to enjoy.*

1 TIMOTHY 6:17 (ESV)

I FOUND MYSELF IN a real pickle. Thankfully, God is a Master Pickle-Fixer.

I raced home in our borrowed car and ran up the stairs to my magnificent kitchen. It was a wonder—a chef's dream. A couple of pastors from our new church wanted to meet with us in our home. In true Beverly Hillbillies style, we'd loaded up the truck from the Midwest and moved into a California mansion complete with a cement pond!

We were fresh out of college, and part of a missions experiment in lifestyle evangelism. Like MTV's *The Real World*, but with Jesus. We were flat broke, waiting on my husband's first paycheck. To say my cabinets were bare was an understatement!

After a thorough search, I found a box of Lipton, a bag of sugar, three gently aging cucumbers, and a bottle of distilled white vinegar. Oh, and a partial sleeve of butter crackers! It would have to do. The sweet tea came together quickly and cooled in a beautiful crystal pitcher that came with the house. My great-grandmother's cucumber and onions recipe—without the onions but with the addition of some dill weed growing wild outside—fit the ingredients.

I put the dish in the freezer, hoping they would be cold by the time our visitors arrived. The crackers spread out artistically on the smallest platter I could find still left room for a pretty china bowl of cucumbers.

The table was set for a feast—carafes of ice water, iced tea glasses and long-handled spoons, and tiny china appetizer plates that came with the house. God knew my heart was to honor these pastors. I just had to hope that the little I had on hand would be enough.

I mustered up a smile and greeted our visitors. I played hostess with my sparse provisions while feeling inadequate for the job. Instead of being disappointed by the lack of a nice spread, the two men raved over the tea and the "fancy marinated cucumbers." But more importantly, we had a feast of the heart, sharing for hours with each other about the goodness of God in our lives. In fact, it seemed as if Jesus was there among us, taking my small offering and making it something so much greater.

Who knew that marinated cucumbers were so delicious with a cracker? The God of pickles. That's who.

Father, help me keep my eyes on you and trust you for everything that I need, knowing that you delight in giving us all things to enjoy. You are my source and my security, and all my hope is in you.

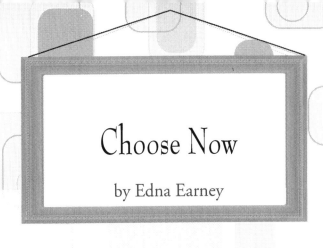

Choose Now

by Edna Earney

Why am I discouraged? Why is my heart so sad?
I will put my hope in God! I will praise him
again—My Savior and my God!

PSALM 42:11 (NLT)

CHOOSE NOW, RIGHT now, whether you will commit to stay married or not."

We were having dinner out with good friends. My husband, Mike, was a rookie police officer, and Mitchell* was his patrol partner. His wife, Tina,* was becoming my best friend. We were two young couples in our twenties.

Tina and I discussed the latest tribulations as police wives. The guys talked shop. I delved into some frustrations when she interrupted, "Choose now." Tina's usual mediating tone became direct. She explained that too many police couples split up, and Mike and I would hit that point also. "It isn't a matter of *if*, it's *when*. If you love Mike and intend to stay married, then choose now, commit now before harder times come."

Hard times came. The reality of Mike's salary as a policeman being half that of his former corporate pay bloodied our budget. I stayed home with our girls because the demands of being a legal secretary while Mike was rotating shifts and moonlighting ran my energy and nerves to their breaking point. Our finances floundered, communication waned, and constant conflict struck hope a death blow.

Mike reluctantly agreed to counseling. At our first session, our counselor let us talk a bit, then asked, "When was the last time you went to church?"

I remember this moment vividly. The question was simple, but waves of emotions swamped me. I realized that I hadn't *felt* as if I'd been to church in years, even though we attended mass sometimes. Where was God in all of this? I had put him in a box for Sunday mass (heard through a squawky speaker in the cry room beside the sanctuary). I lost my relationship with God as I lost my relationship with Mike.

Once a tight spiral, our connection loosened as Mike and I drifted apart and lost intimacy with God. Only God could tighten the spiral with his binding love.

We committed to center God at our core again. With this first revelation toward healing, we saw hope's glow on the distant horizon and felt a warming intimacy long buried in our hearts. The center would now hold.

We lived the range of emotions in Psalm 42:11 that year. We were sad to the point of discouragement, but God led us back to hope—back to praising him! This year, we celebrated forty-eight years of marriage.

*Names changed

Dear God, my Savior, you gave us humans the gift of emotions. But you also gave us a will and a strong mind. Help me overcome making decisions based on emotions in situations. Remind me to center my life on my hope in you, my commitment to living in your sustaining love, especially in times of turmoil.

Wait in Hope

by Lisa-Anne Wooldridge

Be of good courage, And He shall strengthen your heart, All you who hope in the LORD.

PSALM 31:24 (NKJV)

"TAKE ME TO church," I begged my husband. "I need hope." We picked a place at random from the phone book because it was easy to find, and they offered special parking for visitors. Parking is always a challenge in San Francisco, especially when the days are mild and the bay is sparkling blue.

Everyone we encountered welcomed us with kindness. An usher gave us seats at the end of a row because we told him our son was at the children's hospital, and we might need to leave at any time. After three months of living in the hospital and riding a life-or-death rollercoaster, our precious premature baby was finally ready to go home. He was strong, but he'd endured so much. We all had.

Before we could go home, he needed one last surgery—what should have been a simple outpatient procedure. The tiny hernia repair went perfectly, but hour after hour, our son failed to wake up. At first, the doctors weren't worried. But as time went by, they whispered in hushed tones and told us he might never regain consciousness. Devastated, and with a pounding heart, I panicked. I had to get away from the beeping monitors and artificial lights. I didn't want to believe that we'd come through all that just to be disappointed in the end. I needed my baby to be okay.

I'll never forget the words the pastor spoke, almost as if he knew the situation and was speaking just to me. "Be strong, just a little longer. I know your heart feels weak, and you've just about given up. But God will lend you his strength. I know it's hard to wait—but wait in hope! Those who hope in the Lord will never be disappointed."

A small cry of pain escaped from my throat. People in the pews around us put comforting hands on us. They were praying even though they didn't know what we were going through. I felt peace and determination rising in my heart.

I was going back to the hospital, and I was going to take my baby home—now! I was full of hope and resolve. The doctors looked grave, but I didn't slow down. As I walked toward him, my sweet boy woke up and pulled out his breathing tube on his own. He held it up in his tiny fist as if to say, "Let's go home."

Father, thank you for being my strength and giving me hope when all seems lost. Help me to wait in hope for you and to be courageous in the face of fear and doubt. Strengthen my heart and let me overflow with hope!

The Perfect Gift

by Teresa Janzen

*For through the Spirit, by faith, we ourselves
eagerly wait for the hope of righteousness.*

GALATIANS 5:5 (ESV)

I COULDN'T BELIEVE THE prices. Moments before, my daughter had whispered in my ear on the eve of her fifth birthday, "All I want is a Barbie car." Scanning the toy aisle revealed limited options in my price range. I settled on a generic-brand, pink, plastic limo for Barbie and her friends to ride in budget-friendly style.

The next afternoon, dressed in pink lace and crowned with a plastic tiara, she tore into the gift. Grasping the box by both ends, she raised it to eye level. "That's not what I wanted," she whimpered. "I wanted a car for *me* to ride in."

We were both disappointed. She didn't understand the economics of buying gifts in a large family, and I didn't know her expectation. Even if I had known, I wouldn't have been able to give her what she wanted.

Our heavenly Father understands the desires of our heart, and he knows the gifts best for his children. But like little children, we bring our wish list to the Lord without knowing the cost or consequences. We long for happiness, health, and comfort—all good things. Yet the better gift God offers is the hope of righteousness.

God promised the children of Israel he would raise up a righteous branch who would reign, bring justice, and provide safety and security (Jeremiah 23:5–6). God's people rejected his good gifts, seeking to fulfill their desires by taking on the cultural practices of the day.

Even some professing Christ in the New Testament church traded his perfect redemptive sacrifice for enslavement to tradition by seeking approval from religious leaders. It was as if they returned Christ's gift of grace and exchanged it for what seemed more fashionable at the time—righteousness through adherence to the old law.

Could we be tempted to return Christ's perfect gift of salvation through faith and exchange it for something of lesser value? Perhaps we think we can provide for ourselves what we really want. Don't trade your freedom for what you had before: fear, anxiety, hopelessness, self-judgment, doubt, worthlessness, or empty tradition.

God has given you the perfect gift—forgiveness and redemption. Through the Spirit and by faith, you can unwrap and enjoy this gift now and for eternity.

Father God, thank you for the gift of salvation through faith in Christ. Help me desire what you have for me and resist the temptation to look to others for approval. I trust you to know what is best for me. Help me to surrender my expectations and seek your truth alone.

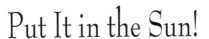

Put It in the Sun!

by Becki James

*Don't envy sinners, but always continue to fear the L*ORD*. You will be rewarded for this; your hope will not be disappointed.*

PROVERBS 23:17–18 (NLT)

I WHISKED THE BLONDE curls into a ponytail before the sticky nectar got them. Holding a peach as big as her face, Kiki stood with juice streaming down both forearms and dribbling from her elbows. With six-year-old ferocity, she attacked the fruit, marinating her nose and joggling tiny glasses up and down with every bite. "Lean forward," I said, angling my torso away from my hips, hoping to salvage another shirt. *What a sight.*

The orchard topped a huge valley. Distant thunder rumbled, and lightning flashed warnings, putting us in high gear to speed up our traditional peach picking with Grandma and Grandpa. I bemoaned the storm, for the Red Havens were gigantic this year. The children seemed unaffected, romping around as usual in a free-for-all paradise.

"Mine's biggest," Micah yelled, darting past his brother with a Jim Dandy raised over his head. I smiled, praising his glory, but knew it would take a while before that green peach ripened.

A moment later, Joel squelched his victory, bellowing, "That one ain't even ripe yet!"

I watched my stepdad kneel, tenderly taking the fruit in his farmer's hands, swirling it through his palms. "Say, that's purdy nice—maybe you just put it in the sun for a bit."

With boyish conquest, Micah turned, chanting, "Put it in the sun!"

Put it in the sun. I mused. *So much like people.*

Recently, I dealt with a sour personality. Unaware, this fellow Christian struggled with pride. On the outside, she held the love of many as an experienced believer. But underneath that ruby appearance, egotism stunted her sweetness. Her words wormed their way into my self-esteem until my spirit gagged. I found myself choking back choice comments, silently spewing distaste to the Lord. *Trust her to me,* he chided, *you just do what I want you to do.*

I knew he was right. I was envious of her popularity and angry at her lack of humility. However, the fruit of others, good or bad, should not arouse discontent. Loving like Jesus meant surrendering her growth to him. And, when I put my sourness under the light of God's Son, he ripened my perspective, awarding me hope.

That king-sized peach went home with us, throned on a bushel basket. We laid it out to ripen at the pace God allotted. I put my envy out before the Son and let him harvest my friend.

Heavenly Father, forgive me when I set my heart to judge. You alone are just. Help me to look at all things under the light of your love so that I am not embittered with envy. I trust myself and others to you. Thank you that my hope in you is secure and that you never disappoint me.

Like Blinking!

by Robin Steinweg

*Rejoice in our confident hope. Be patient in
trouble, and keep on praying.*

ROMANS 12:12 (NLT)

BY THE TIME I visited my optometrist, I had an issue. My work requires hours at the computer. After only one hour, my vision blurs. After two hours, I need a long break in order to focus properly again.

I asked the technician, "What can I do?"

"I have the same problem. It's from dry eyes and not blinking enough because you're on the computer. I was told to blink every two seconds."

I stared at her. "Seriously? You train yourself to blink every two seconds? That's constantly. How is that possible?"

She shrugged. "That's why I use lubricating drops." She suggested a brand to try.

I drove home, the word *constant* beating a refrain in my mind. My daily Bible reading recently included Romans 12:12, which says to be constant in prayer. I'm not sure how many years ago I first read that, but I clearly recall how daunting it seemed. How is it possible to pray constantly?

I knew from watching my mom that it's possible to worry without ceasing. She joked that she worried about worrying and could worry blindfolded with both hands tied behind her back. She worried as automatically as blinking for years! That's the problem. Long, uninterrupted practice had made worry her state of being.

The Holy Spirit taught me several things as I focused on constant prayer. First, don't get in a lather over it. With people, it's impossible, but with God, all things are possible. Second, if he asks me to do it, he'll empower me to do it. Third, I can be aware of his constant presence. I can ask for his help. And fourth, sometimes he puts me in situations that are so pressing they're on my mind continually. Then I have a choice: worry or pray. If I choose to pray, it gradually becomes my default setting, much as worry was my mom's default.

My new prayer setting spills into every corner of my life, fulfilling the first two bits of Romans 12:12. I'll be more patient in trouble, and I'll rejoice in my confident hope.

Constant prayer. Like blinking!

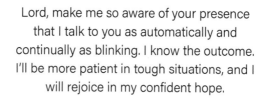

Lord, make me so aware of your presence
that I talk to you as automatically and
continually as blinking. I know the outcome.
I'll be more patient in tough situations, and I
will rejoice in my confident hope.

SNAPSHOTS OF HOPE & HEART

Life in the Past Lane

by Nancy Graves

*And so, Lord, where do I put my
hope? My only hope is in you.*

PSALM 39:7 (NLT)

GREW UP GOOFY. Goofy-foot, that is. It was the 1970s, and skateboarding was sweeping the nation. After getting a skateboard for Christmas, I waited eagerly for the Midwest winter to thaw. When spring finally sprang, my friends and I scouted the neighborhood for the best place to hone our skills. We found it atop the train overpass at the end of my block. The steep incline ran parallel to the tracks, the length of a block and the height of a three-story building.

Youth was on my side. I learned quickly to balance, right foot first, and maneuver my board. Time and again, I sailed over the pitted asphalt and stray stones that threatened my downward and accelerating trajectory. Wind in my hair—me versus gravity—it was exhilarating!

But, like the wind, the years flew by. Decades later, my son took up the sport, and I visited the skate park to watch him and his friends practice their moves. They had half-pipe ramps with copings to drop in from and concrete bowls to whiz around in. Their skills were impressive.

Enthusiasm rekindled, I longed for my glory days. Pushing forty years and carrying an extra forty pounds, I decided to throw caution to the wind as I mounted the skate park bunny ramp. *This will be a piece of cake compared to my three-story plunges!* My son looked on as I assured him boldly, "I got this."

But what I got was what I deserved. Forgetting not only my age but which foot to start on, my weight shifted forward, and I plummeted to the ground like a boulder. Ever heard of a face plant? My cheek caught me. This time it was not exhilarating—it was humiliating and painful! It took over a month for the scar to heal. Me versus gravity didn't work the way it used to. Apparently, I was still goofy—but not just my foot. I had also forgotten, "Pride goes before destruction, and haughtiness before a fall" (Proverbs 16:18 NLT).

Have you ever had an "I've got this" moment? Like me, did you place your hope in past accomplishments and your own ability, only to fall flat? Hoping in anything other than God will bring us down every time. But be encouraged! Placing our hope in him brings a bright future—and an exhilarating ride!

Dear Father, thank you for providing all I could ever hope for in Christ Jesus. Through him, I'm lifted up when I fall down, even if I've caused what made me stumble. Thank you for the peace that comes from hoping in you alone.

SNAPSHOTS OF HOPE & HEART

Fabulous Friend, Fabulous Faith

by Betty Predmore

*As we pray to our God and Father about you,
we think of your faithful works, your loving
deeds, and the enduring hope you have because
of our Lord Jesus Christ.*

1 THESSALONIANS 1:3 (NLT)

WE ALL DESERVE to have that one fabulous friend—the one who brings a ray of light and a sense of joy to your days. I have one such friend. Diana is a true testament to faith and hope. I learn something from her every day.

Life has not been kind to Diana lately. Her daughter has endured months of health issues, resulting in countless trips to the emergency room and numerous hospital stays. Just when they think they are taking a couple of steps forward, something happens to send them ten steps back. The most recent trip to the hospital lasted almost two weeks when her daughter's feeding tube came out of her stomach. She had to be hospitalized while the doctors figured out how to keep her nourished without a nose or stomach tube.

It was such an uncertain time, with several days of no answers, but my sweet friend never lost her faith or stopped praying and trusting God for all the answers.

Through this entire time of fear and uncertainty, I have watched Diana lean into the Lord. It has been my joy to observe her, despite all she is enduring, continuing to give back to others and walking out her faith. She has a beautiful hope in Christ and the acceptance of his will in her life and the life of her daughter. Diana's prayer time is powerful. I've witnessed how she draws great comfort from her conversations with God.

Diana is a true testimony of faithfulness. She is like a beacon on a hill, not letting the clouds dim her shine. Like a lighthouse, she still offers safety to others, even as she endures her own storms.

This beautiful friend is an example of goodness to me, and she has given me hope through my own struggles. My life has been changed by knowing her heart for Jesus, and by seeing the way she trusts God despite the trials.

Many times, we get hurdles thrown at us that seem too high to jump. There are days when the race is too long. I have been a spectator in Diana's marathon, observing as she hands the torch to Jesus and lets him lead her to victory. Because of her mighty faith and unrelenting hope, she will come out of this situation with the heart of a champion.

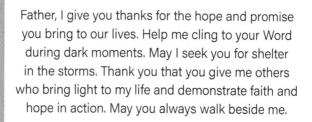

Father, I give you thanks for the hope and promise you bring to our lives. Help me cling to your Word during dark moments. May I seek you for shelter in the storms. Thank you that you give me others who bring light to my life and demonstrate faith and hope in action. May you always walk beside me.

Not Without Hope

by Carin LeRoy

Why am I discouraged? Why is my heart so sad?
I will put my hope in God! I will praise him
again—my Savior and my God!

PSALM 43:5 (NLT)

I WASN'T READY TO lose her. It had been only weeks since I received the news that my eighty-four-year-old mother had liver failure caused by an aggressive cancer. Doctors said she didn't have long to live. She had always been strong, healthy, and vibrant, so this turn of events shocked me. I was distraught as I rearranged my schedule to be with Mom.

On a rare quiet afternoon, we shared a few words together when she told me, "I prayed that God would take me fast."

"Mom, why would you pray that?"

"Because I don't want to be a burden on you kids," she said.

She wanted me to know that God had answered her prayer. She had cared for my father for years and watched his decline into severe senility before he died, and she wanted to spare us that burden. She seemed happy that her journey to heaven would be a short one and that her family was with her.

Early one morning when I walked in to take care of her, she asked, "Why is this taking so long?"

I almost giggled at her impatience. She was ready to go, even excited that she would see her Savior soon.

My time with her passed in a blur, and in just thirty-three days, my mom was gone. Her sudden death put great sadness in my heart—even depression. I expected her to live much longer, like her mother. Yet, I was blessed that she had been the mentor and friend that all daughters need. Her absence created a huge sense of loss for me. What would my life be without her?

We will all experience times that bring us devastating sadness, especially when we lose a loved one. We may withdraw for a time as our hearts grieve and recover from the pain. But God never wants us to stay there or wallow in it. Life may never be the same, but God equips us to continue our life with purpose.

God's Word says we will not grieve like people without hope (see 1 Thessalonians 4:13). This earth is our temporary home—heaven is our forever one. We can praise God for the wonderful gift of eternal life to those who die in Christ. We are not without hope. One day, we will see our loved ones again. What a day of rejoicing that will be!

Father, thank you that as your children, we have the hope of eternal life. In loss, comfort me with that truth. One day when my journey on earth is done, I will see your face, all the glories of heaven, and the loved ones that went before. I praise you today that there is always hope when we know you.

A Weighted Hope

by Kristine Accola

This hope is a strong and trustworthy
anchor for our souls. It leads us through
the curtain into God's inner sanctuary.

HEBREWS 6:19 (NLT)

WHY IN GOD'S aqua-green ocean would we want to be weighed down by an anchor? Have you ever thought about how heavy and burdensome that would be to carry? Goodness, we carry enough weight each day. We don't need an anchor. On the other hand, maybe we do.

I love to go barefoot everywhere. But there are some places where my feet can't go. Like rocks, hot pavement, and climbing mountains—unless I add weight to my feet with shoes. There are these new-fangled products called weighted blankets to help people sleep better. People also cuddle them. They are designed to calm the anxieties of the day.

Paperweights are used so that the thousand-word essay you wrote for class doesn't blow out of the window. I learned that one the hard way. How about those little weights you put on the bottom of helium balloons so they don't fly into the wild blue yonder before your five-year-old's party even starts?

There are other kinds of weights in this world that are a bene-fit to our lives rather than a detriment. These weights give us hope for the outcome. Think about an anchor on a ship. It's meant to secure that ship. What happens if a ship has no anchor and starts coasting off into the unknown or into stormy weather?

Some of my storms, I'm sure, could have rivaled the Bermuda Triangle. What if the ship comes loose in the harbor, and it drifts out of the dock and crashes into another boat? Oy! Can you imag-ine that insurance call?

Picture God as our captain, us as the ship, and Jesus as our anchor. Jesus keeps us attached to God and lets us go to him in the captain's quarters (inner sanctuary) because he is already there. He is the anchor to our soul. Our hope is in trusting his promise that we are safe, secure, and sheltered. He keeps us in a safe harbor, a welcome port in the storm.

When the winds and crashing waves want to tear our sails and batter our boards, let's take heart and have hope that Jesus is our anchor. The weight of this hope is because of Jesus's bless-ed *assurance*, which is better than *insurance* because his blood and righteousness cover everything. Paid in full. With no deductible.

Dear Jesus, I often feel like a ship off course, being tossed about in the middle of choppy waters. Thank you for being my anchor, for being my hope during the storms of life. You shelter me in a safe harbor that I can always call home.

Hearts Will Turn

by Edna Earney

No, the LORD's delight is in those who fear him,
those who put their hope in his unfailing love.

PSALM 147:11 (NLT)

MISTIE DISCOVERED THAT her haunting feelings of not quite belonging were justified. The man she called Dad for over forty years was not her biological father.

She emailed me through a genealogy website, saying her DNA test matched us as relatives. Intriguing! As our family genealogist, I was excited to help her find the connections. My family comprises many adopted children, including those by birth adoption, blended families, and foster care adoption. My husband, Mike, met his birth mother only the year before Mistie contacted me. These images revved my researcher's engine as Mistie provided information.

Her mother's fuzzy memory of her long-ago liaison included details describing my brother Jim. I called him to broach the sensitive subject. He was confused and understandably hesitant. "I didn't even live in our hometown then. I couldn't be her dad. Even so, why would she contact me now?"

My excitement sputtered. *Why would she contact me now?*

rattled my brain. I replied cautiously. "Well, she is looking for her father, seeking closure. She wants to know the truth."

Competing emotions pulled at me as Jim requested I "drop it" and stop email conversations with Mistie. Honoring his decision, I told Mistie we reached a dead end, and she would have to look elsewhere. My heart broke for her desire for the family connectedness our other adoptees have embraced.

I knew I could help connect the pieces. I stewed about it, figured the angles, and fitted words to imagined emails. But my actions would honor neither my brother nor God and could lead to disaster. I prayed, asking the Lord to melt my brother's heart, knowing only God could make a human heart move. Psalm 147:10 says God does not find pleasure in *our* strength, then counters in verse eleven, saying he does find pleasure as we stand in awe of him and trust his unfailing love. God was the answer, not me!

God did soften my brother's heart. A year later, new information, a DNA test for Jim, phone calls, and a tearful resolution ensued. Our families celebrated together as Jim met Mistie in person recently. Jim is making up for lost time, sharing hundreds of stories and pictures. Our family has expanded again.

When we trust in God's unfailing love, mountains will move. Chains of bondage will break. Mired feet will spring free from quicksand. And fathers' hearts will turn to their daughters.

Dear Lord, thank you for your steadfast love. Help me turn immediately to you, not counting on my own strength, but standing in awe of you and trusting in your perfect, eternal love for me.

Manna Mindset

by Kelly Herr

*Lead me by your truth and teach me, for
you are the God who saves me. All day
long I put my hope in you.*

PSALM 25:5 (NLT)

AS I DROVE past the place I loved, feelings of rejection flooded my mind. Not wanting to develop a root of bitterness, I decided to try something different. I prayed for them.

This place I loved was the small Christian school where I grew up and taught for sixteen years. My dad helped build it, and I attended classes there. After I married and had children, I taught while my children were educated there. My dream was to one day be principal. Three times I tried, and three times I was rejected.

While my husband chased job opportunities out of state, I earned my master's degree, and we landed back home. Now more qualified, I tried again and was again not chosen.

God provided a teaching job that required driving by my beloved school twice a day. Passing by brought an oppressive pain to my heart. I knew I couldn't continue to bear this hurt, so I turned to God, seeking his truth. He led me to pray for my school and be thankful for the job he provided. He was meeting my needs, although I preferred to be elsewhere.

Before long, I looked forward to driving by. Gratitude filled my heart as I prayed for this school I loved and for the school where I then worked. I realized God had a plan. His truth taught me his ways are higher than mine. He sustained me throughout the year as I prayed every day, never expecting to gain my heart's desire.

When the school year ended, the principal's position unexpectedly reopened. With hands shaking, I tendered my resume to the director. Those old feelings of rejection wanted to resurface, but I trusted God's plan. Either way, he was my provider. His truth had changed me.

This time, God allowed me to become principal, and I am grateful—grateful to serve and equally thankful for the truth God taught me in the trial.

In Exodus, as the Israelites traveled to the land God promised them, they complained when food supplies dwindled. God heard and daily provided them bread from heaven called manna. But instead of being grateful, they complained. Like the Israelites, I had to learn again to give thanks for the manna he provides.

Every day I depend on him. Every day he saves me. My hope is in him.

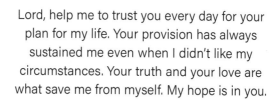

Lord, help me to trust you every day for your plan for my life. Your provision has always sustained me even when I didn't like my circumstances. Your truth and your love are what save me from myself. My hope is in you.

God Is My Hope

by Sandy Lipsky

*Therefore, we who have fled to him for
refuge can have great confidence as we
hold to the hope that lies before us.*

HEBREWS 6:18 (NLT)

*T*HE DOOR TO the waiting area opened with a thud. The
nurse who escorted my daughter to the examination room
stood in the doorway. She held the doorknob until our eyes met.
Releasing her grip, she hurried in my direction. "There's a problem
with your daughter's EKG." She sounded worried. "We detected a
malignant rhythm."

My only child had complained of chest pain on a walk a week
prior. This wasn't new. As a four-year-old, she'd experienced the
same thing. A specialist at that time determined her heart was fine.
Nothing to worry about.

Now almost a decade later, we thought it wise to re-evaluate.

I tried to understand "malignant rhythm." Malignant sounded bad. Fear welled inside my chest. The nurse continued. "Her
QT rhythm is long." Her voice shook as she spoke. Not good.

We left the office dazed. What began as a simple stress test
had turned into a life-threatening concern. With a prescription in

hand and a number to call, we exited the building. The nurse's final words, "Nighttime is the most dangerous for this type of rhythm," haunted me.

Because of the reputation of the specialized cardiologist, our appointment wasn't for weeks. I didn't sleep. I snuck into my daughter's room every night to check her breathing. I resigned myself to a hopeless outcome. One evening I wept in our bedroom, tears dripping onto my hands. My husband entered the room and stood next to me. "Have you prayed for God to heal her?" he whispered.

His simple words felt like a cool breeze on a blistery day. How could I have missed the obvious? God is my living hope. He loves me and deserves my trust. I had accepted the diagnosis as a death sentence instead of running to my heavenly Father for help.

Immediately my prayers changed as if a lightbulb switched on in my spirit. Hopeful confidence replaced resignation. I began sleeping again. When our appointment arrived, peace came with us. Whatever the news, we were in his hands.

When the cardiologist shared the test results, we rejoiced. Although her QT rhythm was longer than normal, it wasn't "malignant."

A miracle? Maybe. But I was reminded nothing is hopeless with God by my side.

Father, you care about the details of my life. So often I try to handle circumstances on my own. Help me remember to bring everything to you. There is nothing too big or small. You are my living hope.

Joy in the
Journey

by Vickie Price Taylor

*Faith shows the reality of what we hope for; it is
the evidence of things we cannot see.*

Hebrews 11:1 (NLT)

MY DAUGHTER'S DOG Bella and I love taking trips together. She enjoys nothing more than a nice car ride followed by a long walk. Last summer, we went out almost every weekend for a "splore" (our doggy word for *explore*). Her excitement and anticipation levels are genuine and expressive.

The fifty-pound rottweiler-shepherd mix bounds off the couch, rushes to the door, and looks up to me with a sparkle in her eyes, a sweet doggy smile, and a body all but vibrating with eagerness. Such unabashed joy warms my heart.

Though she has no idea where we're going or how long it will take to get there, she's eager for the adventure and confident of the outcome simply because she's with me. In her guileless doggy way, she's expressing both love and trust.

Oh, how I wish I could be more like Bella as I face the many adventures life brings. Often, when circumstances spin me in a new direction, or a different door of opportunity opens, I step back, cautious of what might jump out at me. Or I cower in the corner, afraid to take a single step because I can't fully see what's on the other side. I'm afraid of making a mistake and worried I'll wander off in the wrong direction. Where have my enthusiasm and confidence gone? Would Jesus address me as he did his disciples? "Where is your faith?" (Luke 8:25 NLT).

Hebrews 11:1 explains that "faith shows the reality of what we hope for" and the "evidence of things we cannot see" (NLT). This verse adds voice to Bella's actions. Together, they remind me that the hope I have amid the twists and turns of life is found in my Master, the one who calls me to follow him regardless of where the road heads. Because of his steadfast love, I can trust him to lead me beside still waters and restore my soul.

Joy is available in the journey, regardless of the destination, because he directs my path.

Father, thank you for guiding my steps.
Help me remember that you know all my
days, and I do not need to be afraid. Remind
me to place my hope in you and face
each new circumstance with confidence,
knowing you are right by my side.

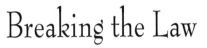

Breaking the Law

by Mary Curcio

For the law never made anything perfect.
But now we have confidence in a better hope,
through which we draw near to God.

HEBREWS 7:19 (NLT)

I KNEW IT WAS wrong, but I had to have that five-cent candy bar. Even if I got caught, what could they do to a little eight-year-old girl? My heart pounded as I looked around the store. Quietly, I leaned against the shelf and slipped my favorite candy bar into my pocket.

Fear and guilt gripped me after eating it. I had tried to talk myself out of stealing it. I reasoned—it was only five cents. I felt so guilty, I couldn't get to confession quick enough. I poured my heart out to the priest. I heard him say, "You are forgiven," but I felt no peace. I broke the law and knew God would punish me.

God doesn't want us to be afraid of him. His Word says to draw near to him as a little child, but I still feel as if I'm not good enough. I try to be good, but I mess up. I still think I have to "be good" so God will hear my prayers. My mind knows he loves me regardless, but my heart wavers between being "good enough" or accepting his truth. It's like being on a teeter-totter wondering if I will fall off.

I thought I had to be perfect, but stealing that candy bar showed me I wasn't. Even though I want everything I do to be flawless, it doesn't give me more favor with God. Learning to place my faith in him rather than in my own efforts, I have new hope. I don't have to earn his favor. I now know he is the only one who can remove my guilt.

Do you ever dwell on your past behavior? In those days of rebellion, my heart sought other pleasures rather than him. Although I still remember stealing that candy bar, I don't dwell on it. Guilt from my past no longer haunts me. My peace comes from knowing that "there is now no condemnation for those who are in Christ Jesus" (Romans 8:1 NLT).

No one can be made perfect by following God's rules—the Old Testament law. Instead, the law in the Bible reveals our need for a better hope in Jesus. I once hoped if I were perfect, God would accept me. But now, knowing the sacrifice the sinless Jesus paid, I draw near to God as a child to a loving parent. My heart is at peace.

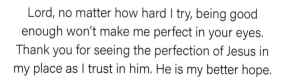

Lord, no matter how hard I try, being good enough won't make me perfect in your eyes. Thank you for seeing the perfection of Jesus in my place as I trust in him. He is my better hope.

SNAPSHOTS OF HOPE & HEART

I Will See You There

by Denise Margaret Ackerman

*So that being justified by his grace we might
become heirs according to the hope of eternal life.*

TITUS 3:7 (ESV)

I WILL NEVER FORGET that day. My husband and I were tearing the weathered shingles off our roof when my mom called with terrible news. My father's condition had deteriorated, and the doctors felt he only had twenty-four hours left to live. It had been two days since I visited him after his surgery. He was in pain, but I had no idea how grave his illness was.

I rushed to the hospital, overwhelmed at the thought of losing my beloved father. Burdened for his salvation, I prayed that God would give me the right words to say. My dad believed in God, but his need of a personal relationship with Jesus was foreign to him.

Once I arrived at my dad's bedside, the serious nature of his condition was evident. On morphine, he was in and out of consciousness. I silently prayed God would give us time alone when dad was alert. He seemed aware each time a family member arrived and when they left.

The moment finally came when Dad and I were alone. It was time for me to leave, and I wept as I tried to form my parting words. Dad told me not to be sad.

I replied, "I just want to know that you will go to heaven."

Dad said, "That's not up to me."

I told him he could know *for sure* he had eternal life if he would ask Jesus to forgive his sins and invite him into his heart. Dad offered no response but once again fell asleep. I waited by his bedside until he woke up.

Dad's farewell reply to me is forever etched in my heart. "If I'm not here tomorrow, you know where I'll be, and I will see you there."

My dad's bedside conversion is a beautiful comfort to me. God answered my prayer! I have a confident, joyful hope knowing I will see my dad again in heaven. There wasn't time for Dad to accomplish great things as a believer, yet because of God's grace, he became an heir of eternal life that night. Dad's place in heaven was secured the moment he placed his faith in Jesus.

How marvelous that we are saved by the grace of God and not by works that we have done (see Ephesians 2:9).

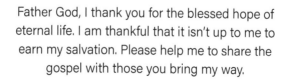

Father God, I thank you for the blessed hope of eternal life. I am thankful that it isn't up to me to earn my salvation. Please help me to share the gospel with those you bring my way.

Waiters Wait

by Robin Steinweg

I wait for the LORD, my soul waits,
and in his word I hope.

PSALM 130:5 (ESV)

WHY ARE WAITERS called waiters? I don't see them wait. They're on their feet from the moment they clock in until their shift ends.

For example, meet Jodi, my family's favorite local waitperson. During our dinner out, we marvel as she greets and seats customers, wipes the tables, and dispenses menus. Sails off and returns with ice water. Skims past to deliver steaming coffee cups.

Our model server materializes to take the meal order. She rattles off specials, salad dressing choices, and dozens of desserts. Listens carefully—memorizing—not even stopping to write it all down. When the food is ready, here she'll come, a hefty tray of meals balanced on one hand while plates are set in front of the correct diner—all without spilling a crumb.

Minutes later, we hear her voice. "Steinweg family, how's the food? No, you can't hide your green beans under the napkin. Eat them."

Multiply these actions by Jodi's number of tables. The only

other professionals I know who multi-task like this are pipe organists and drummers, hands and feet flying every which way.

I never understood why waiters are called waiters until my husband and I dined at a five-star restaurant. The elegant atmosphere charmed us. But it was our personal waiter who made the evening memorable. He stood out of our line of vision around a corner but kept us in view. He placed napkins on our laps. Watched our meal's progress. Refilled our water glasses often and whisked away our salad plates a beat after we swallowed the final forkful. We'd barely finished chewing the last of our meal when finger bowls of lemon water appeared with steamy cloths. He was as attentive to us as if we were royalty. He *waited* on us!

In the faith life, waiting isn't rushing around doing as many things for God and others as I can. It's also not sitting around watching the clock or the calendar, wondering if God will ever answer my prayers.

It is watching for God's move. Paying attention to his ways. Waiting means listening for his Spirit, ready. Ready to respond quickly when he nudges me. I place my hope in his Word, which is how I come to know what he's likely to want of me. My actions follow.

My whole being quivers with the anticipation of hearing from him and serving him. I want to be God's waiter!

My Lord, I wait on you. With an eager heart, I have hope—confidence—that my waiting will result in the privilege of serving you. I want to pay such close attention to you and your Word that all you have to do is look in a direction, and I'll go there. I wait for you, my King!

SNAPSHOTS OF HOPE & HEART

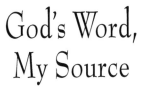

God's Word,
My Source

by Eva Burkholder

*You are my refuge and my shield; your word is
my source of hope.*

<small>PSALM 119:114 (NLT)</small>

HAT'S WRONG WITH me?" I asked my husband. "I have no motivation to work. I only want to do macramé all day. Is it hormones, aging, or this pandemic?" He embraced me and let me dampen his shoulder with my released emotions. Weary and losing heart, I wanted to retreat from life and its many struggles.

Dreaming of a safer world, I longed for all to experience health. I desired family members to reconcile and people to be polite and kind. And I wanted my children to follow Jesus until the end.

While these hopes are normal and acceptable, I recognize that nothing in government or science can guarantee they will be achieved. Furthermore, my favorite author, most respected speaker, and even my husband are all helpless in fulfilling my hopes.

But God, my refuge and shield, instructs me to hope in his Word. Not in the actual ink and pressed-wood sheets of paper, nor the ritual of daily devotions, or study, or even memorization. My hope is in the almighty creator God who lifts off the pages as I read the written words.

Other Bible translations tell me to "put my hope in" God's Word. I like this because it implies an act of my will. I take my hope, that's typically in politicians or my bank account, and I deliberately transfer it to God. My false sources of hope do not have the power to deliver, but God's guidance and boundaries are trustworthy. His promises and truths spoken on the pages of the Bible will not disappoint.

After a good cry, I opened my Bible and found the perfect hope for my despondent soul. "And let us run with endurance the race God has set before us. We do this by keeping our eyes on Jesus, the champion who initiates and perfects our faith" (Hebrews 12:1–2 NLT).

Where do you go for your source of hope? Whatever your need, open the Book that defines true hope. You will find your answer, as I did.

Jesus, thank you that when life is hard, I can open your Word and find hope. Answer my cries. Show me again and again what is true. Bring hope to my soul as I seek you in your Word.

Hope Floats

by Vickie Price Taylor

I know the LORD is always with me. I will not be shaken, for he is right beside me. No wonder my heart is glad, and I rejoice. My body rests in safety.

PSALM 16:8–9 (NLT)

*T*EARS STREAKED DOWN my face and blurred the tree lights into a kaleidoscope of colors as I curled up on the couch in the predawn hours. My body was tired, my mind weary, and my heart broken. My husband was unemployed, I was working two jobs, we were both struggling with depression, and Christmas was only days away. I was so exhausted I didn't think I could move and so overwhelmed I felt as if I would drown.

"Help me, Lord," I prayed. "I can't do this anymore." At that moment, I felt completely bereft and desperate for someone to truly see me and come to my rescue. And someone did.

In those quiet, solitary moments, I felt God's presence so keenly it was as if he sat right beside me. Without a doubt, I knew he was there, comforting and soothing me.

I didn't sink beneath the waves of heartache and discouragement because God showed up when I needed him most. I was able to rise from the couch and prepare for the day, not because my circumstances had changed, but because my perspective had.

Moments like this one create a sort of mile marker in our walk with the Lord, and each one draws us closer to God and helps guide us when we face the next difficult situation. I am currently in one of the most challenging seasons of my life, and I have repeatedly cried out to God, just like I did that morning years ago. His gentle response is the same. His Spirit gives me peace, his Word gives me guidance, and his people offer me support.

I know it is his faithfulness that helps me face each new day and allows hope to float above the storm. My heart may break, and my body may fail, but because Jesus is with me, my spirit can soar.

Faithful Father, I am so thankful you never leave me. Because of your love and compassion, I can count on you to lift me out of the darkness and into the light. Stay close to me today as I face what lies ahead and keep me safe in your loving arms.

Keeping Hope in Focus

by Kristine Accola

*But I will keep on hoping for your help; I will
praise you more and more.*

PSALM 71:14 (NLT)

*A*S I WRITE this, I could name a dozen things that are going wrong in my life. I'm weak with discouragement regarding finances, health, and relationships. Instead of dwelling on these problems, I need to look back on all the times in my life that God salvaged.

I can choose where I fix my gaze. I gain hope when I focus on the moments that God modified and the attitudes God adjusted. In addition to being a feeling, hope is a choice.

It's okay not to be okay. But we can't stay there because down and out is enemy territory, and the devil will come looking to destroy us. During seasons of hardship, we need to look for and expect deliverance *every* time, even when the situation *takes* time. Even before he rescues us, we can praise God because of the hope he planted in us through each past hardship. We have "pictures" of each experience in our memories. And each time we experience another answer to prayer, it fuels our hope in him. It is perpetual. With God in our viewfinder, our direction is driven by hope.

When I start to lose hope, it's because I'm focusing on the wrong thing, looking down at my circumstances instead of up at my Creator. "We are hard-pressed on every side, yet not crushed; we are perplexed, but not in despair; persecuted, but not forsaken; struck down, but not destroyed" (2 Corinthians 4:8–9 NKJV). Why not? Because of hope.

From the time we are born again until the day he calls us home, we benefit from refocusing and renewing our hope in him. It is continual and everlasting. God has released us from our past and given us a hope for our future.

Each time God changes a situation, or more often, when he brings me through one, it gives me renewed hope and victory. When I see the differences it makes in my life, I'm encouraged to trust in God even more while things aren't as clear. Right now, I need to wipe my faith lenses and sing God's praises anyway.

So, when you feel helpless, focus on hope and sing hallelujah!

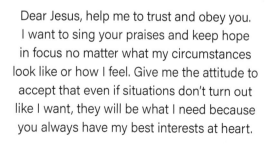

Dear Jesus, help me to trust and obey you. I want to sing your praises and keep hope in focus no matter what my circumstances look like or how I feel. Give me the attitude to accept that even if situations don't turn out like I want, they will be what I need because you always have my best interests at heart.

SNAPSHOTS OF HOPE & HEART

The Serenity Sponge

by Mindy Cantrell

*Let all that I am wait quietly before God, for my
hope is in him.*

PSALM 62:5 (NLT)

HERE ARE TIMES when my brain flits around at break-
neck speed, worrying about every little matter in my life. It
seems that for each concern, I need to plan out the perfect scenario
to the nth degree. Once done, I begin to second-guess myself. As a
result, I am an anxious mess. Sound familiar?

When I let myself go for days, soaking in this worry mindset,
I often end up with a migraine. With an expensive trip to the ER
and a few days of recovery afterward, it is a colossal waste of time
and energy! So, why do I continue to sop up all this worry, knowing it will cause more trouble? Good question.

In my mind, the desire to be in control overrides the quiet
voice of truth. The truth that tells me I'm not really the one in
control, but rather, I am being controlled by fear. Yikes! I finally
realized that in my guarded need for control, I become a casualty
of the Enemy, who wants to negate my testimony, rendering me
useless in God's kingdom.

How about you—do you feel a need in your life that dampens your usefulness? I have discovered a sure-fire way to counteract these destructive needs—being quiet before the Lord. This takes a little practice, but once learned, it empowers our usefulness and soaks us in serenity.

What does it entail? For five minutes, an hour, or on and off for days, sitting or lying quietly, speaking, or singing praise, put yourself in timeout. Let go of outside distractions. Lie face-down on the floor if you need to. Concentrate on God. Tell him how you love him and thank him for loving you. Ask the Holy Spirit to envelop you in his presence. Be still and feel it.

If your mind wanders, pull it back with praise. Declare, "Holy, holy, holy, is the Lord God Almighty!" Worship your Creator. Let go of your fears, allowing the miracle of his unending love to lift you. Bask for a time in the redeeming presence of your Savior and be renewed.

Whenever I take time out to sit before God, with all my mind, body, and soul, I am quieted. I am sustained. My need for control diminishes, and I have restored hope that everything is going to be okay.

Dear heavenly Father, thank you for loving and sustaining me, even during my crazy bouts of destructive needs. Please help me sit quietly before you, like a sponge, soaking you up and then wringing out the worry I no longer need. Help me rest in you alone, every moment of every day, as I place my hope firmly in you.

Mud Run Ready

by Hally Wells

*So prepare your minds for action and exercise
self-control. Put all your hope in the gracious
salvation that will come to you when Jesus
Christ is revealed to the world.*

1 PETER 1:13 (NLT)

HAT DOES A lazy Sunday countryside with live music, a cold beverage, and compadres have remotely in common with a torturous physical challenge in cold, damp conditions while fellow "soldiers" wail in pain?

Seemingly, nothing connects these, but something does. In rural eastern Missouri, there's a well-known venue—with barns, vineyards, dining, and breathtaking backdrops—a coveted wedding venue and a soul-soothing place to spend the day making memories. However, that same venue doubles as the "battleground" for a well-known mud run held each fall and spring.

It was for that memory-making and injury-inducing event that I, presumably of sound mind, registered with members of my church small group. Five couples, ages thirty-five to fifty-five, gathered that rainy October day to tackle balancing, jumping, and climbing obstacles covering a three-mile stretch of manufactured mud, made sloppier and heavier with lots of help from Mother Nature.

In our group of ten, I held rank. The second oldest, I was

nudged out by my older half. Without calculations, I felt confident I measured up in the body fat category. I *know* I won gold for most athletically and coordination-challenged among my mud-running teammates. With matching T-shirts—ours read "Baptized in muddy water"—and our trustiest, crustiest tennies, we posed and posted, clipped and contained hair, and talked pathetic smack before getting in line.

In thirty seconds flat, I established my position in back. The group was encouraging, but my meaner half pulled me—like arm almost out of the socket—through the mud, determined for us not to get left behind. While I vigorously attempted most "activities," I appreciated the "go-around" option. I worried about falling from the rappelling wall, but falling face first in slimy, slippery mud was the bigger threat, particularly since my bad knee might have popped out at any time.

When Meanie and I rounded what seemed like the trail's one thousandth turn, a friendly young man shouted a reassuring "age is just a number." Sometimes, it's best to say nothing.

In the end, with jellified muscles and solidified embarrassment, I resolved that if I ever attempted a mud run again, I'd prepare. Diet. Exercise. Counseling. The basics.

We prepare for runs and weddings, interviews, and travels. Do we ready ourselves for life's most meaningful marathon? Are we prepared for the spiritual battles and obstacles awaiting us? We should be. There's not a race nor challenge more important!

Almighty God, fill me with the discipline and motivation that I need to make right choices each day. May they leave me ready and equipped for your coming on that glorious day.

SNAPSHOTS OF HOPE & HEART

My Only Hope

by Denise Margaret Ackerman

Behold, the eye of the LORD is on those who fear him, on those who hope in his steadfast love.

PSALM 33:18 (ESV)

*T*HERE'S NOTHING ELSE we can do. It's in the Lord's hands now." I was five months into a complicated pregnancy. The twins weren't viable yet. Medical attempts to stop the premature contractions failed. A feeling of desperation swept over me as the doctor turned and walked away.

In the lonely stillness of my hospital room, my heart remembered what happened in this same hospital two short years ago. We had stood in the intensive care unit, praying for our two-week-old son, Christopher. Born two months premature, our firstborn baby fought valiantly in a battle he did not win.

Now, like a seismograph recording volcanic activity, the bedside monitor recorded the rise and fall of my steady contractions. Even with medical advances, could my babies survive? How much longer before they were born? My mind flooded with uncertainties. All I could do was wait and pray.

My friend Barb had asked the Lord to give me another son to help me heal from the pain of Christopher's death. Not long after her prayer, I was overjoyed by a positive pregnancy test. I had been certain God had answered Barb's petition. Certain, until hearing the doctor's words.

As a young believer, I faced a mountain-sized test of my faith. I knew God loved me. I knew he heard my prayers. I knew he was my only hope. So, I placed my worries into his loving hands. With childlike faith, I surrendered the outcome to him.

After my prayer, I drifted off to sleep. At some point during that night, the contractions stopped. No explanation—no medical intervention—just stopped. A few days later, I was released from the hospital and spent the next several weeks on bed rest. The babies waited to arrive until four weeks before their due date.

Our healthy twin sons recently celebrated their fortieth birthday. I still marvel at the miracle the Lord gave us! Since that frightening hospital stay those many years ago, my hope has been shaken countless times. I am still learning that trials are easier to bear when I release my worries to the Lord. His plans for me are good. I can place my trust in him because he is worthy. He gives me hope when I rely on his steadfast love for me.

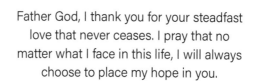

Father God, I thank you for your steadfast love that never ceases. I pray that no matter what I face in this life, I will always choose to place my hope in you.

A Light for
Your Path

by Mary Harker

*Such things were written in the Scriptures long
ago to teach us. And the Scriptures give us hope
and encouragement as we wait patiently for
God's promises to be fulfilled.*

ROMANS 15:4 (NLT)

*T*HE TWO SOMBER travelers plodded along the hot, dusty
road. Their leader, the rabbi, was gone. Discouraged and
disillusioned, they processed all that transpired over the last few
days. The future was uncertain and bleak. What was the hope of
Israel's redemption now?

Deep in conversation, they didn't even notice him at first, a
stranger that joined them. He seemed oblivious to all the recent
happenings. How could he not know? Then he chastised them for
their unbelief, for being slow to see and understand. He began
the most significant teaching of Moses and the prophets they ever
heard. Their hearts and eyes were opened with his instruction.
Words they heard numerous times before now became a balm to
their hurting souls. Could it be the Messiah had risen and walked
with them as he said? Did they dare hope?

✧

Like these sojourners on the road to Emmaus as told in the Bible,
I am slow to hear and believe the promises in God's Word. Several

years ago, our family was devastated by a failed adoption. Our hopes rose like a bubble in the air then suddenly burst out of sight. This began a dark season of my soul. But my tears fell like rain on seeds of renewed faith over time. The Lord reminded me of the Scripture, "Jesus wept" (John 11:35). Those two little words brought hope and illuminated the truth that Jesus understands my pain and walks beside me along the darkest path. Emmanuel. God with us.

The words of the Bible are treasures to be mined. They bring hope and promise to our hurting souls if we take the time to read them. Even five minutes out of a busy schedule can change the focus of the day. God's love and redemption plan, the precious blood of Jesus, weave like a scarlet thread from Genesis to Revelation. When we are on a difficult road, the Word of God lights our way in the darkness. His Word is a lamp for our feet and a light for our path (see Psalm 119:105).

Father, thank you so much for the gift of your Word. I hold on to your love and cherish the plan of redemption woven through all of Scripture. When the way is dark, your letters of love shine truth and light my path.

Out from Under the Covers

by Charlaine Martin

*And endurance develops strength of character,
and character strengthens our confident hope
of salvation. And this hope will not lead to
disappointment. For we know how dearly God loves us.*

ROMANS 5:4–5 (NLT)

*U*GH! I HAVE so much to do," I grumbled, waking up from a nap I didn't want to take. Chronic pain and fatigue sideswiped my day—again.

My struggle began at the peak of my fitness career several years ago when I woke up feeling as if a truck hit me. *How can I do my job as a lifeguard and water instructor?* I trudged to call off work at the YMCA. A few hours in the pool were impossible. My doctor eventually diagnosed me with fibromyalgia, while autoimmune disease lurked in the background.

This new reality prompted me to finish my bachelor's degree. My family needed my financial support. What a struggle it was to work, help at church, and finish my studies. I wanted to quit, but my family cheered me on. When life became tougher, I wanted to pull the covers over my head. Yet, God gave me hope through classmates and loved ones who applauded my victories. Tears trickled down my face when I finally walked onstage to receive my degree.

One day, a pastor's wife in my exercise class asked me, "Char, what is God doing through your illness?"

I thought for a moment. "God gave me the ability to do so much. What he gave me, he certainly can take away." Her question redirected my thoughts, *I must honor him in all I do because all I do comes from him.*

I learned to trust that he will carry me through because I have hope. My exercise class members persevered when they showed up on bad days. They inspired me to keep showing up too. I developed deeper compassion for people suffering from similar conditions. Some found inspiration to persevere through my example by trusting God daily, finding hope.

The apostle Paul inspired the Roman church by pressing through challenges and encouraged them to do the same. God grew their character as they persevered in trials, which gave them hope. We all face difficulties, but hiding under the covers isn't the answer. We can face whatever comes because nothing is impossible with God, who gives us strength.

What trials tempt you to call it quits? Cry out to God, who loves you. He will carry you through those challenges until glimmers of hope shine through. Simply move forward step by step, praising God for your victories. You might encourage others to do the same.

Lord, I can't make another move or take another step on my own. This trial is too much for me. Please help me keep going when I want to quit. Pick me up and carry me through. I give you all the glory, honor, and praise. May others see you in the victories you give me every day. Thank you so much!

A Father's Legacy

by Darla S. Grieco

I say to myself, "The LORD is my inheritance;
therefore, I will hope in him!"

LAMENTATIONS 3:24 (NLT)

"I JUST WISH I had realized." The regret in my loved one's voice spoke to the depth of her sadness. Her father-in-law had passed away the week prior. He lived several states away, and as the clean-out process began in the decedent's home and office, the man's adult children uncovered a treasure trove of blessings that escaped their awareness during his life.

From awards to government commendations, this humble man never broadcast to his family the amazing successes he accomplished in his work life. The time and energy he invested left a unique thumbprint upon the world in his field of business. He passed along a legacy for his children and grandchildren in the form of a financial inheritance. "Now that I see what he has left us, I just wish I had known so I could sincerely thank him," my loved one lamented.

Most fathers here on earth work hard to build up an inheritance or bestow a legacy for their children out of pure love for their families. They do not care to receive any accolades in return. However, a mere man can only build up a reputation or a bank account. Our heavenly Father, on the other hand, has built for you an eternal home in heaven with him. The inheritance he has prepared contains a promise of ongoing relationship—of love, peace, patience, joy, and eternal salvation through Jesus Christ.

Unlike my loved one's grief, when it comes to receiving the Father's legacy, you need not waste time mourning. There's no reason for crying out later, "I wish I had known." Instead, choose to receive your inheritance today by giving your life to Jesus. He loves you. You are precious to him. All you need to do is accept the truth that Jesus Christ died for your sins and came back to life. Acknowledge your sinful past and grant him acceptance and permission to reign over your future days. Are you ready?

Heavenly Father, you've given me such an amazing gift in Jesus. Thank you for the access I have to receive my inheritance today. I repent of walking through life without you and freely welcome you into my heart and life, that I might walk with you all of my days.

SNAPSHOTS OF HOPE & HEART

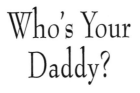

Who's Your Daddy?

by Sally Ferguson

*Lord, sustain me as you promised, that I may
live! Do not let my hope be crushed.*

PSALM 119:116 (NLT)

*G*RA'MA, WHO TOOK care of you when you were a baby?"
I could picture the mental wheels clanking into motion
as little Sophea pondered the complexities of life.

"My mommy and daddy." I pointed to my dad, sitting across
the room.

Eyes wide, Sophea said, "Grandpappaw is your daddy?"

A few minutes later, not derailed from her original train of
thought, Sophea tried again. "But who took care of them when
everybody was a baby?"

Oh, the wonder of a child's mind as we see the world from
her height.

Yet, it gave me pause. We did begin, maybe not at the same
time as Sophea imagines, but we were all dependent on someone
to provide for our needs. Do we ever outgrow the necessity to be
nurtured, cared for, and protected?

I think back to my dad's upbringing. His father died of a brain tumor when Dad was in his teens. His grandfather emigrated by himself from Sweden when he was twelve years old. Generations of children have had to navigate the passages of life on their own, but were they ever really alone?

We have a heavenly Father who tends his flock, gathers the lambs, carries them close, and gently leads (see Isaiah 40:11). I cherish that thought, knowing my grands are in his safe care.

The older I get, the more I am aware of my inadequacies in measuring up to life's expectations. I need my Abba, Daddy, to sustain me in the storms and boost my hope when all looks bleak.

And you know what? God has never failed me. In darkness, he is my lamp. In storms, he is my lighthouse. In sickness, he is my physician. His promises never fail. He will take care of little Sophea too.

Thank you, Lord, that I don't have to question your provision for me. Your timing is perfect, your character impeccable. I know you are faithful and true. Help me teach those qualities to my grands so they will walk with you in confidence and strength. May they see your light of hope when darkness surrounds them. You are our life-sustainer.

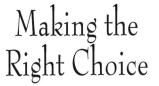

Making the Right Choice

by Annie Wolter

*Blessed are those who trust in the LORD and have
made the LORD their hope and confidence.*

JEREMIAH 17:7 (NLT)

MR. WOLTER, I'M sorry to tell you that the colonoscopy revealed cancer. We're sending you for an ultrasound this afternoon to determine the stage and develop a game plan." As the doctor explained the details to my husband, I teared up. What was happening? Can my forty-four-year-old husband really have colon cancer? Is he going to die? We had married two years previously, and the "in sickness" part of our wedding vows had already become a reality.

By the end of that day, we knew he had stage two cancer—the malignant cells had spread into the wall of his colon. He would undergo chemotherapy and radiation, followed by surgery. Weeks later, the medical team successfully removed several inches of his colon and determined that nearby lymph nodes were cancer-free. But a risk remained that tiny undetectable particles had spread to lymph nodes and would lead to trouble. So, Paul had to choose whether or not to receive an additional type of chemotherapy post-surgery to reduce the likelihood cancer would return.

His doctor sympathized with the difficulty of deciding whether to take the extra chemo or refuse the chemo to avoid the risk of permanent neuropathy that could result. Paul found research indicating the extra chemo was only beneficial to people of an age and health condition he didn't fit. He didn't want to take the extra chemo.

But still, he wanted to *know* the right choice. He prayed ardently, "Lord, I need your help. What should I do? Chemo, or no chemo? Which path do I take at this fork in the road?"

After three weeks of seeking God's wisdom, Paul heard God's clear response—and it surprised him. He sensed God answer, "I'm with you on either path." There was no right or wrong. Paul was free to make the choice and know the Lord would remain his hope, his confidence, and his constant companion throughout the highs and lows of life. Paul made his choice and let it all go into the hands of God.

Seven years later, he remembers God's response. Paul knows now, more than before the ordeal, any challenge he faces is a new opportunity to hope and trust in God.

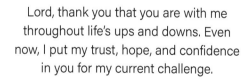

Lord, thank you that you are with me
throughout life's ups and downs. Even
now, I put my trust, hope, and confidence
in you for my current challenge.

Members-Only Perks

by Dorothy Mae Spradley

Blessed be the God and Father of our Lord Jesus Christ! According to his great mercy, he has caused us to be born again to a living hope through the resurrection of Jesus Christ from the dead.

1 PETER 1:3 (ESV)

*D*O PLASTIC TABS clutter your keychain? Or have you graduated to an app for storing all your memberships? I appreciate a special program to safely store all my money-saving perks. While most memberships include immediate bonuses, some members-only perks roll out after the criteria is met. I get a bit impatient waiting for my rewards to add up.

You may be wondering, "What does this have to do with Jesus?" Look closely with me at today's verse. While praising God, the apostle Peter rejoices at the start of this letter because God "has caused us to be born again to a living hope." See that word *us*? Those two letters represent all of us who have placed our trust in Christ. What a membership group we belong to!

When connected to Christ, we experience a change in our priorities that alters how we think and live. We live to please God. We long for more than this moment and the pleasures of this life. To be born again, to be part of Jesus, connected to him, includes so much more than any other membership. This truth provides both an immediate reward—Christ within—and something well worth waiting for—victory over death.

For the recipients of this letter from the apostle Peter, that was good news. This persecuted group of first-century believers risked their lives telling others about a risen Savior who beat death. It's no wonder that Peter began this "How to live hope filled when your life is threatened on the daily" pep talk with an expression of gratitude. Gratitude helps us recognize God's preservation, even during hard times.

What's more, when Peter adds "to a living hope through the resurrection of Jesus Christ from the dead," he highlights how a connection to Christ trumps any difficulty, including death. The resurrection, Jesus's empty grave, displays his power over death. Through being born again and united to Christ, that same power is ours (see 1 Corinthians 15:53–57).

When we come to Jesus, we sign up for the greatest perk of all time. It's true. A relationship with the risen Lord allows us to face life's hardships with undying hope. Christ's presence dwelling within gives us living hope for today. Then, we can also look forward to our own future victory over death.

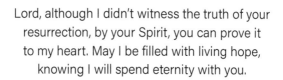

Lord, although I didn't witness the truth of your resurrection, by your Spirit, you can prove it to my heart. May I be filled with living hope, knowing I will spend eternity with you.

Heart

The Designer's Heart

by Mindy Cantrell

Guard your heart above all else, for it determines the course of your life.

PROVERBS 4:23 (NLT)

REMEMBER THAT TIME when you desired something so deeply, your whole heart ached for it? For me, that heart-achy time of yearning revolved around gorgeous, cutting-edge fashion.

My whole being longed to be able to dress in haute couture style every day. I spent every free moment pouring over *Elle*, *Vogue*, and *Cosmopolitan* magazines, devouring the tiniest details. Each unique button, gold zipper, metallic thread, padded shoulder, and wonky heel set my soul aflame! I scoured name-brand discount stores, spending every spare penny, that I might flourish these same scorching details.

The compliments I received on my appearance boosted my self-confidence. I prided myself for my high style on a low budget. I was happy, having reached my dream, my heart's desire of being fashionable and pretty.

Then God showed me my attitude—my *heart* attitude. I had succeeded in dressing myself in fine fashion but had begun to quietly judge those who didn't. It seemed all I noticed was what someone was wearing, if their hair and makeup were styled, if their shoes and handbag were trendy, and if their accessories were just right. Much of the time, I would miss what someone said because I was too busy dissecting how they looked.

Deep in my spirit, it hurts to admit that I traded the honorable details of God's spiritual fruit within me for pride and designer labels. One day I caught myself in harsh thinking of a beloved friend because of what she was wearing. I rushed to the ladies' room in tears. I confessed to God my haughty attitude and asked him to help me change. And you know what? He did.

I will admit some days remain a struggle. I still notice what everyone is wearing. However, the difference now is that I cover my thoughts with God's love. Daily, I fill my heart with what really matters—God's Word. My mind's judgments are transformed. Now, with God's love inside me, the physical imperfections fade, and the unique beauty God placed within each person becomes radiant and clear. My redesigned heart is truly happy, for there are no character details more haute couture than the characteristics of God.

Are you in need of a heart redesign today? May I recommend you take it to God—the kindest and most fashionable designer of all.

Dear God, I confess, again and again, my need for your perfect love to transform my wayward thoughts. Please fill my heart with your fruit of the Spirit— love, joy, peace, patience, kindness, goodness, faithfulness, gentleness, and self-control. May they redesign and determine the good course of my life.

When God Opens the Door

by Denise Margaret Ackerman

But the LORD said to Samuel, "Don't judge by his appearance or height, for I have rejected him. The LORD doesn't see things the way you see them. People judge by outward appearance, but the LORD looks at the heart."

1 SAMUEL 16:7 (NLT)

*M*Y EMPLOYMENT HOPES faded as soon as the elevator doors closed. My resume showed a four-year gap. I lived fifty miles away. And when asked if I had questions about the job, my response was, "How much time off do I get?" What a ridiculous question to ask a potential employer. Mr. Snyder would surely hire someone more suited to the position at his prestigious downtown office.

But I really needed *this* job, and I needed it soon. We had enrolled our three teenagers in a private Christian school located a few miles beyond the downtown office. The office schedule would align with the hours that our children were at school. It was a leap of faith because paying the tuition was beyond our reach unless I found a well-paying job.

Doubt filled my heart because I didn't feel polished enough to be chosen. The more I tried to imagine myself fitting in at this beautiful office, the more inadequate I felt. If I had conducted the interview, I certainly would have hired someone else.

Thankfully, the long car ride back home gave me time to reflect on the bright aspects of the interview. I enjoyed speaking with Mr. Snyder, and overall, I had been relaxed and open with him. We discussed the four-year break in my work history, during which time I had home-schooled our children. We talked about my previous office positions and the promotions I received at each company.

By the time I pulled into our driveway, I had decided to leave the outcome in the Lord's hands. He opened the door for our children's enrollment at the school, and he was able to provide the necessary finances.

A week later, I received the call offering me the position. Joy bubbled up as I accepted it, so thankful that Mr. Snyder did not judge me as harshly as I had judged myself. There may have been better-qualified candidates for the position, but I was relieved that the Lord opened the door for me. Not only did he use me despite my weakness, but he blessed my heart as I sought to do his will.

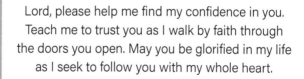

Lord, please help me find my confidence in you. Teach me to trust you as I walk by faith through the doors you open. May you be glorified in my life as I seek to follow you with my whole heart.

A Heart of Worship

by Natasha Lynn Daniels

Draw near to God, and he will draw near to you. Cleanse your hands, you sinners, and purify your hearts, you double-minded.

JAMES 4:8 (ESV)

MY PRECIOUS LITTLE girl, Vicka Adele, was born in Ukraine to a birth mother who drank while pregnant with her. Her mother gave birth to her at home while drunk and left her to die. Due to these circumstances, she suffered a stroke at birth on the left side of her brain, leaving her with the right side of her body non-functioning and a diagnosis of cerebral palsy.

She is a very high-functioning little girl who exudes joy and never complains about life. She teaches her daddy and me so much. She inspires others around her with how she loves Jesus and worships despite her circumstances. Vicka Adele loves to sing and worship our Savior all day long. It doesn't matter if we are at home, in the car, in the store, getting our nails done, or at church; if she feels the Spirit, she will sing loud and draw near to Jesus wherever she is.

One morning, Vicka's song was gone. She began having uncontrollable seizures and was unable to walk, talk, sing, and dance. We needed answers. Approaching Jesus in anguish, I begged him to heal her and cried out, "Please don't take her." The Lord heard me and drew near to me.

After a long stay in the hospital, the doctors finally established the right combination of medicine. Vicka Adele's song was back, and we were able to return home. The most rewarding gift of all was when we assembled again at church.

Tears slid down my face as I watched Vicka Adele waste no time worshiping her Savior. She sang loud, danced before the Lord, and lifted her hands in praise to him. It had been a while since she'd been able to do that. Her daddy and I smiled and felt blessed to watch her—so openly and without shame—worship the one whom her soul loves.

In James 4:8 we are encouraged to trust God and be comforted by him. When we posture our hearts to Jesus, we lay aside our circumstances and shift our focus on him. With clean hands and a pure heart, we humble ourselves before him during life's trials and sense his presence.

Let's draw near to Jesus with praise in the store, in the car, in the nail salon, in the church. Let's cleanse our hands and purify our hearts before him wherever we are.

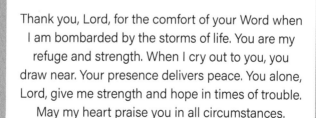

Thank you, Lord, for the comfort of your Word when I am bombarded by the storms of life. You are my refuge and strength. When I cry out to you, you draw near. Your presence delivers peace. You alone, Lord, give me strength and hope in times of trouble. May my heart praise you in all circumstances.

What Have I Done?

by Darla S. Grieco

*Let us go right into the presence of God with
sincere hearts fully trusting him.*

Hebrews 10:22 (NLT)

AVE YOU EVER done something terrible that you knew
you'd have to report? I'll never forget the day I backed into
my husband's car. When my babies were young, I would sneak off
just before sunrise to enjoy a quick game of tennis before the little
ones awoke. The sun and I would arrive at the courts about the
same time. Perfect!

However, on the morning I mentioned, the pre-dawn darkness and the angle of my car blocked my husband's vehicle from
view. My excitement to head out to my playdate, coupled with the
incline of my driveway, necessitated I gun it to get going. *Crunch!*

Entering into my husband's presence that morning to confess
what I'd done left me feeling sick in my stomach. Would he be
angry? Would he admonish me? I'd understand if he did. However,
I already felt frustration and disgust in my own heart, and certainly didn't need to come face-to-face with *his* disappointment. This

mistake would cost us time and money. But I couldn't avoid it. Regardless of his response, I had to face him and confess.

Unlike approaching a human, we can freely enter God's presence without fear of his response to what we need to confess. What a blessing! He fully knows that as we walk in our humanness, we will make mistakes, yet he doesn't condemn us. Furthermore, being omnipresent, he already knows our wrongdoings and the yearnings in our hearts, no matter how impure they might be. Nothing we say or do surprises God.

Our times of confession and coming clean before God are for our benefit, not his. He provides us a loving space to accept responsibility for our past choices and gain wisdom for our future ones. So, I encourage you, don't hold back when you enter into God's presence. He longs for you to come near to him. You can fully trust him with your pains and confessions, and in his safety, you will find grace and forgiveness.

Enter into his presence today with a repentant heart. You can trust him with anything you might need to share.

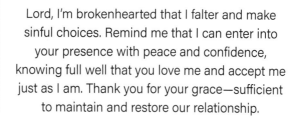

Lord, I'm brokenhearted that I falter and make sinful choices. Remind me that I can enter into your presence with peace and confidence, knowing full well that you love me and accept me just as I am. Thank you for your grace—sufficient to maintain and restore our relationship.

A Heart Makeover

by Joanie Shawhan

*A peaceful heart leads to a healthy body; jealousy
is like cancer in the bones.*

PROVERBS 14:30 (NLT)

"IT'S NOT FAIR!" I railed at the Lord, tears streaming down my cheeks. Once again, I witnessed the prayers I had pleaded for myself transform into answered requests for another person. When will it be my turn? The shards of shattered dreams I grasped so tightly cut deep into my heart.

For too many years I grieved over what I felt should have been mine. In my grief and disappointment, I stumbled into the pit of jealousy.

When I realized Scripture compared jealousy to cancer in the bones, I shuddered. As an ovarian cancer survivor and nurse, I recalled viewing the X-rays of my oncology patients. Cancer had gnawed moth-eaten patterns of holes in their bones and destroyed their structural integrity. Had jealousy, like cancer, breached the integrity of my heart?

Comparing my circumstances with the lives of others often triggered bouts of jealousy. I focused on my loss as if I had slipped my grief under a microscope and magnified my lack. My scope of vision narrowed until I no longer recognized, let alone appreciated, the blessings and gifts God had given me. The anger, self-pity, and resentment spawned by jealousy drained my energy, strength, and peace.

My heart needed a makeover. Maybe it was time I magnified God instead of magnifying my disappointments. As I thanked and praised God, he opened my eyes to the blessings he had given me, including my own unique purpose and calling. He enabled me to rise out of the pit of jealousy, healed my broken heart, and restored my health and peace.

Over time, I realized I'm grateful God did not answer some of the prayers I prayed. Those answers would have robbed me of my destiny and the joy I now experience.

As I grappled with the disappointment of unanswered prayer, God transformed my heart with peace.

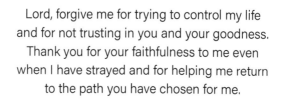

Lord, forgive me for trying to control my life
and for not trusting in you and your goodness.
Thank you for your faithfulness to me even
when I have strayed and for helping me return
to the path you have chosen for me.

My Heart, His Home

by Gina Stinson

Then Christ will make his home in your hearts as you trust in him. Your roots will grow down into God's love and keep you strong.

EPHESIANS 3:17 (NLT)

*H*OME. TO SOME, home is merely a place to crash after an exhausting day at work, but from the time I was a young girl, I dreamed of creating an inviting home. As a child, I first demonstrated home design by the way I played with my Barbies. I never owned one of those fancy, multi-story Barbie houses. Instead, I created my own one-story suburban home using Lincoln Logs to outline the perimeter of the ranch-style residence. I made furniture from random items around the house. Barbie could easily splash in her pool made from a repurposed salad bowl.

As I grew older, I watched my mother take extra time to create a hospitable and welcoming home. She repurposed antiques, set a beautiful dinner table with mismatched dishes, freshly poufed the pillows on the couch, and made sure the house sparkled. She created an atmosphere of casual elegance and refreshment. From the well-manicured flower beds to the sweet aromas from the kitchen, guests felt the effort in the inviting atmosphere.

As a Christian, I crave an inviting heart atmosphere. I want an open invitation welcoming the presence of Jesus. I want Jesus to feel at home in my heart—a heart decorated with love, joy, and peace. Like an honored guest in my home, making Jesus feel welcome in my heart-home might involve special, extra-mile acts of kindness and hospitality. I may forgo my preferences for his—after all, his way is best.

Years ago, I invited Jesus to make his home in my heart. The struggle to keep a pure and clean heart, where he would feel most at home, has been difficult. I confess there have been many remodels. I've hoarded bitterness, hurts, and unforgiveness. But God, in his love and mercy, keeps cleaning me up, purifying my heart, and sanctifying me. He's growing my faith and strengthening my roots. He's redefining spaces and places in my heart so that when they are completed, they will reflect his beauty and hospitality.

What a masterpiece he's creating! It is a beautiful privilege to welcome Jesus as my guest and my friend for eternity.

Lord Jesus, I am humbled and grateful that you reside in my heart. Please help me to keep it a place where you feel welcomed and at home. Purify my motives, my actions, and my words. Thank you for wanting to make my heart your home.

My Forever Home

by Joanie Shawhan

Wait for the LORD; be strong, and let your heart
take courage; wait for the LORD!

PSALM 27:14 (ESV)

M Y MIND GALLOPED as I explored the possibility of homeownership after years of apartment living. My real estate agent and I waded through multiple listings. Eventually, we narrowed our search to the condominiums where I sensed the Lord's leading.

We viewed several condos with my list of requirements in hand: a pool, a satisfactory layout, second floor, and sunny. But none were quite right.

One day, we walked through a unit with a southern exposure, and my breath caught in my throat. I stared at the up-to-date décor, the built-in shelves, and a third bedroom twenty-three feet long in which I envisioned rows of floor-to-ceiling bookcases.

Even though the condo was on the first floor, I forged ahead to make an offer. But the more I prayed, the more my chest tightened. Peace eluded me. As much as I desired that condo, I needed to let it go. This wasn't the unit God had planned for me. I swallowed the hard lump in my throat and told my agent, "Not this one."

Anticipation mounted again when a second-floor unit in the same building became available. My heart raced as I arrived at my possible new home. I walked through the door, and my eyes swept the room. But the unit listed a higher asking price, needed a makeover, and the anticipated library proved non-existent. My shoulders slumped as I turned and walked away.

Months went by with no scheduled viewings. Would I ever find my forever home?

One day, my real estate agent sent me information about another condo: second floor, southwest exposure. I hadn't seen my real estate friend for a while, so I thought it would be fun to get together. I scanned the photos, but they didn't impress me.

We met at the condo for what I considered a perfunctory walkthrough. When we stepped into the master bath, I gasped. The pattern of the wallpaper border was a near-perfect match to my shower curtain and bedspread. I felt joy bubble up inside. This was the condo God had chosen for me. It emboldened my heart to take courage.

I purchased the condo. But I was unaware of another surprise God had for me: a panoramic view of fiery sunsets brushed with shades of pink, peach, and lavender. What a beautiful gift God had given me.

I waited for the Lord, and he gave me his best.

Lord, you are so faithful to me. Thank you for showing me the value of waiting for you and for sending your peace as a confirmation of your will. When I wait for you, you give me more than I could ask or imagine.

Lodestone Living

by Nancy Graves

You're blessed when you get your inside world—
your mind and heart—put right. Then you can
see God in the outside world.

MATTHEW 5:8 (MSG)

*A*S I LOOKED around, I was struck by a wonderful thought—*We're all here because of Jesus!*

It was spring in Chicago, and I heard on the local Christian radio station that an Easter service was scheduled in one of the downtown office buildings not far from where I worked. Excited, I looked forward to going.

The day finally came! I rode the elevator up to the top floor conference center. The capacity crowd milled about the room, greeting one another and finding their seats. There was an array of people: some young, some old, and certainly, from diverse backgrounds.

What a departure from my usual corporate experience. It wasn't a strange sight in itself to see a packed conference room in a Chicago office building. That happened every day. But this wasn't just any group. Gathered together were lifelong Christ-followers, those starting out in their faith, and some hoping to feed their curiosity. We each responded to the event promo and made our way through the surrounding metropolis up to this place. Like the pull of a magnet, we were drawn to come. This otherwise common space had become holy ground. What a beautiful sight!

It reminded me of the Sermon on the Mount, over two thousand years earlier. The townspeople in northern Israel came from far and near. The rich and poor, the young and old. All were welcome. They left what lay below to follow Jesus up the mountain because something in him had spoken to something in them. Their minds and hearts were drawn to the truth, and wanting more, they came to sit at the feet of the Teacher.

Likewise, this day in Chicago, the skyscraper we ascended stood as an urban mountain. We, too, left what lay below, magnetically drawn by *the* Truth—Jesus, our lodestone.* Our minds and hearts wanted more. The Teacher turned Savior was still speaking—to us. It was so good to sit at the feet of the Word of God.

Have you ever seen the commonplace turned sacred? Like me, were you amazed at the goodness of God to reveal himself in an unexpected way? In his presence is fullness of joy (Psalm 16:11). Together, let's praise him for drawing us near through the magnetic-like force of Jesus.

*A lodestone is a piece of magnetite or other naturally magnetized mineral, able to be used as a magnet.

Oh, Lord, I praise you for drawing me into your presence. I want to be near you. Your words are life and peace to me, the guiding truth I need. Please help me to see you all around me, every day.

Heart Strong

by Kelly Herr

*My health may fail, and my spirit may
grow weak, but God remains the strength
of my heart; He is mine forever.*

PSALM 73:26 (NLT)

A TENNIS FRIEND SAID, "Some people have bad days, some bad weeks, some bad years, and some bad decades." At that moment, I felt I was experiencing the latter. I was only in my twenties, but my family had many health issues.

I tried to do everything right by raising my family, working hard, and helping my parents. I went to church, volunteered, and worked out daily, but those weren't enough either. I prayed for miracles and waited for answers I thought would never come.

Mom had schizophrenia. My husband stroked out during unexpected heart surgery, which paralyzed him for months. Then my brother and dad both died of cancer. My favorite Bible character was Job because in the end, God restored him. If God blessed Job double for his troubles, then that's what I wanted.

But God didn't allow the victory yet. Right after my husband learned to walk again, I discovered I had melanoma. I was only twenty-five with a two-year-old son! As I waited for surgery to determine whether I'd live or die, I lay on the floor and cried out to God. *I can't take care of everyone if I have cancer. I've always taken care of my health! God, why haven't you taken care of all these things for me? I'm trying so hard to please you!*

In those desperate days of waiting, I read my Bible like never before. The Scriptures strengthened me even though I was scared. The Word steadied my soul. My heart grew stronger. Although I couldn't see the miracle, I saw the bigger picture. I went into surgery knowing God was with me, and I trusted his plan.

In Psalm 73, Asaph described his grieved heart. He tried hard but didn't prosper. Even worse, he became bitter because the wicked were prospering. He wondered, as I did, if all of his efforts were in vain. Then he realized his final destination. Our hearts and health may fail, but as believers, our home is heaven, eternal glory.

The cancer had not spread, and I received my miracle! During this trial, I learned where my strength comes from. God does give us physical strength, but spiritual strength is more important. We will have many hardships in this life, some physical like cancer, some mental and emotional, and some spiritual like doubt. But don't give up, dear Christian. He is our strength and source of happiness and blessing. He is ours forever.

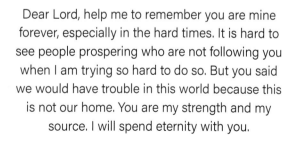

Dear Lord, help me to remember you are mine forever, especially in the hard times. It is hard to see people prospering who are not following you when I am trying so hard to do so. But you said we would have trouble in this world because this is not our home. You are my strength and my source. I will spend eternity with you.

Supernatural Transplant

by Robin Steinweg

*You were cleansed from your sins when you
obeyed the truth, so now you must show sincere
love to each other as brothers and sisters. Love
each other deeply with all your heart.*

1 PETER 1:22 (NLT)

I WAS A ONE-GIRL posse, champion of the underdog. Can
you picture it? The skinniest girl in class confronted peers
picking on another kid—"Cut it out! Let her go!" Surprisingly,
they did.

I pitched into a fellow eight-year-old, with fists flying, when
the boy swung a poor kitty by its tail. "How *dare* you?" The cat
escaped. The boy cried.

I broke into a thicket of football players who pushed and
slapped a smaller kid—reached up-Up-UP to grab the collar surrounding the trunk of neck on the largest of them and shouted,
"Leave him alone!" I could have been squashed like a gnat, but the
tree-like youths only laughed. They let both of us go.

That was me. Rescuer of the underdog—and in one case, the
undercat. I held my own court of justice, acting as arresting officer,
eyewitness, prosecuting attorney, jury, and judge. Privately, I de-
spised those in snobbish cliques and hated those who treated others badly. Some of my actions may have appeared commendable,

though I could've been more—well—diplomatic. But my heart was black with hostility and loathing for people.

In church, I'd hear, "Love your neighbor like you love yourself." How could I love such rotten people, I wondered. It seemed so natural to hold others in contempt. I tried, though. Gritted my teeth and tried to force myself to love them. I couldn't even work up to a little *like*.

One evening, a friend shared with me truths about God's love. About Jesus's sacrifice for all sin. If I opened the door to him, he'd forgive me and come into my life to stay. What I wanted more than anything was to belong to him and be more like him. The instant I opened myself to Jesus, my hating heart surged with God's love and light.

In fact, he removed that heart. In a spiritual transplant, he exchanged my faulty heart for his heart of love. Where my natural tendency had been intense dislike, he made it possible to do the opposite. Possible even to love my enemies and bless those who mistreated me.

His Word urged me forward on a new path. One of sincere and deep love. Full-out, nothing-held-back love. A love only made possible by a supernatural heart transplant.

Lord, I'm continually amazed at your unlimited love and how you made a new person of me. I might be tempted at times to scorn people for their hateful acts. But you remind me that the heart you put in me is designed to hate sin, not people. Let it be so! Thank you, Lord of my heart!

An Honorable Heart

by Gina Stinson

But in your hearts honor Christ the Lord as holy,
always being prepared to make a defense to anyone
who asks you for a reason for the hope that is in you;
yet do it with gentleness and respect.

1 PETER 3:15 (ESV)

IN INNOCENCE, SHE answered the question. There was no hidden agenda, no ill-intentions, no secret motive. In her heart of hearts, her words were never meant to hurt anyone. But the listener turned her words into hateful, jealous, and pre-meditated communication. In moments, her honest response became tangled shrapnel in a war of words. The natural response would be to protect herself—to get fired up and defensive. Her emotions soared.

Our words have power. In this modern world, people are quick to react. Whether you intend for your words to hurt or not, it's possible an unassuming conversation with a friend or acquaintance can be twisted or misunderstood. This trend silences not only conversations but relationships. Freedom vanishes when innocent words are misrepresented—twisted to fit an agenda.

Visible only to God, our hearts reflect our motives. We can't control how others respond to our words, but we do control how we deliver and respond with our words. Do my words reflect the holiness of the Lord? Do they deliver the message of hope that is within me? Can I defend my words with gentleness and respect? These questions help me determine the intentions of my heart.

I know in my own life I have misused and abused words. The motive of my heart magnified myself and minimized the reflection of God's beauty and holiness. Thank God and others for their forgiveness. But forgiveness isn't a license to ignore my responsibility.

What great privilege we have to be an outward reflection of inward purity and gentleness. What if my words spurred conversations that encourage more talk of hope and holiness? What if I took the time to quiet my emotions when frightened or challenged by someone's response? What if I learned to distribute hope with hard conversations?

Preparing my defense depends on the motive of my heart. When an opportunity to answer for myself develops, I hope to speak with a pure heart. Without hesitation or apology, then I can confidently proclaim the hope we have in Jesus. Aligning my heart with his words fosters a message of hope and healing our world needs today.

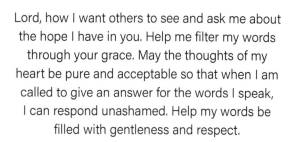

Lord, how I want others to see and ask me about the hope I have in you. Help me filter my words through your grace. May the thoughts of my heart be pure and acceptable so that when I am called to give an answer for the words I speak, I can respond unashamed. Help my words be filled with gentleness and respect.

Getting Personal

by Edna Earney

The purpose of my instruction is that all believers would be filled with love that comes from a pure heart, a clear conscience, and genuine faith.

1 TIMOTHY 1:5 (NLT)

*G*OOD TEACHERS RELATE to their students. Sometimes they get personal. I surprised my senior English students with facts about me in stories that revealed my humanness. After all, I was once a teenager and had my own *oopsies* in life.

I told them about one attempt at the Presidential Fitness Test. I watched the coach measure distances starting at twenty feet, demonstrate an underhand throw, and hand the softball to the first girl in line. My turn came. I toed the chalked line, hesitated, then tossed an overhand throw that plopped down ten feet away.

The coach reminded me to toss underhanded and passed me another ball. I focused, tossed underhanded with all my might, watched the ball spin high up—into the sun—and thud about ten feet away. Too bad they weren't testing for height. Coach called, "Next!" I shook my head and lined up for the next embarrassing event.

My students chortled at that one. They also appreciated that I wasn't a 4.0 student. I was proud of my B in Algebra II because

I attended tutorials to earn that grade. I missed being an honor graduate by two-tenths of one percent.

Although I knew about Jesus from an early age, I didn't make him Lord of my life until my late twenties. Students related to my near misses and couldn't-quites. Those stories made them feel better. They saw a successful, honored teacher in front of them and realized my reputation wasn't dependent on mastering everything in life but on the intervention of a faithful God. He saw the girl with scrawny arms and continued to teach her.

Likewise, I imagine Timothy following his mentor, Paul, who wrote him a letter of encouragement that became part of Scripture. Though Paul was Timothy's spiritual father with an awe-inspiring reputation, Paul readily admitted he was a sinner saved by God's grace, as Timothy was. Paul charged him to teach others of Christ's love—"love that comes from a pure heart" and a "clear conscience."

Can we achieve those ideals? Yes, if we confess our short-comings to clear our conscience and accept God's sacrificial love that purifies our hearts. Maintaining a clean heart and clear mind draws our focus to God's abilities, not ours.

As I admitted my human inadequacies to my students to point them to God's transformational power, I prayed they would understand what Paul taught: biblical love centers on genuine faith in God, not on false faith in ourselves.

Dear almighty God, please help me be transparent to others. Create a clean heart in me, and keep my faith centered on you as my source of knowledge and understanding. Thank you for being our source for all good things.

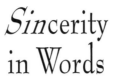

Sincerity in Words

by Darla S. Grieco

May the words of my mouth and the
meditation of my heart be pleasing to you,
O LORD, my rock and my redeemer.

PSALM 19:14 (NLT)

*A*POLOGIZE FOR WHAT you've done!" Those words escaped my lips more times than I could count during my sweet babies' younger years. Having had four precious children in a five-year span allowed for frequent squabbles and infractions. Demanding an apology for careless behavior became my go-to line.

Though my little darlings usually complied with my request by speaking the words I asked them to say, sometimes, the furrowed brows and crossed arms of the guilty party conveyed a different message entirely. Often, I could see the words spoken through stubborn lips were not consistent with the recalcitrant heart's disposition.

Truth be told, I catch myself in this same type of predicament far too often. In my humanness, I behave in ways that are not consistent with my heart—or vice versa. Emotions kick in, and I respond without thinking at times, my knee-jerk reactions inconsistent with how I know I should behave. Or my remorseful heart might cry out, recognizing I've made a poor choice. Yet, in my stubborn nature, I refrain from allowing my words to express the shame and regret for what I've done. Could it be my sinful nature is interfering with my ability to be authentic?

As the psalmist mentioned, these two areas—our words and our thoughts (the meditation of our heart)—sometimes lack consistency, and we must pay attention to both, especially when we come to the throne of God. Why bother trying to come before him with insincere words when he already knows what is in our hearts? There is no need to be fake with God. He sees all and knows our every word before we speak. He created each of us in our mother's womb and accepts us inside and out (Psalm 139:13–14, paraphrase).

As I continue to grow closer to God by studying his Word and by spending time in prayer, I understand which behaviors and attitudes align with his expectations. God's pure and intense love leaves me longing to please him. What better reason to get my head and heart in agreement so the words I speak will be pleasing, reflecting a heart for him.

Lord, teach me how to honor you in all I do and say. So many impure thoughts try to seep into my mind, leading me astray. Help me to filter the meditation of my heart and my words so they might be pleasing to you.

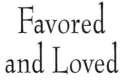

Favored and Loved

by Becki James

For we know how dearly God loves us,
because he has given us the Holy Spirit to
fill our hearts with his love.

Romans 5:5 (NLT)

HE TIME HAD come. The child that moved within her for nine months was forcing his way out of her. Locking her elbows, she propped herself up until her shoulders dropped forward and her chin fell to her chest. Gulping a moment of rest through parched huffs, she watched the child distort the shape of her abdomen one last time. It frightened her—God, himself, was within her. Yet, she recalled the angel's words, *Mary, do not be afraid. You have favor with God.* She was to bear the Son of God, and his arrival was upon her.

The first sounds of God's voice filled the room as the tiny babe cried out the salvation of mankind. Jubilation crushed Mary's pain as God announced his presence. She opened her arms and cradled him to her chest, which, all at once, seemed full to bursting with emotion. His cloudy eyes fluttered to open, searching to connect with her. In an instant, all was still.

With his first glimmer of sight, the infant hushed her own soul as though he knew her terrified joy. *Emmanuel, God with us,* she breathed against her fingers. God was here.

ᕫᕎ

I like to think I ponder things as Mary did. Mary's commission to carry and care for God's Son was something she bore for the rest of his life. Even as a human mother, she had to be mindful of God's presence. Did she ever forget she lived alongside God? Did he remind her with that same tender glance? Just as Jesus came to dwell with mankind, so God the Spirit remains with us, filling us with his love. I wonder how often I forget he is God, even though I bear his presence? He stays with me. Am I listening for his voice to fill my heart?

Sometimes life leaves me breathless. Sometimes I am frightened that God lives within me. I feel far too flawed, until I recall the purpose of his cross. Jesus left his throne as the Son of God—to become the son of a teenage girl—so that I might be a child of the King. All at once, I fall silent as one dearly loved. God is here. The cross cradles me with forgiveness, and the Spirit embraces me with his loving presence.

Fall silent. Look to the cross. He loves you dearly.

Dear Holy Spirit, thank you for never leaving me. Thank you for walking beside me and living within me so that I am filled with your love. Please be my constant companion. Help me to live like I know you are with me.

SNAPSHOTS OF HOPE & HEART

The Best Refuge

by Nancy Kay Grace

No wonder my heart is glad, and my tongue shouts his praises! My body rests in hope.

ACTS 2:26 (NLT)

I RECEIVED A PHONE call from my oral surgeon after a tongue biopsy. "I've got bad news and good news. The bad news is that it's cancer. The good news is that we got it all."

My mind froze at hearing the word *cancer*. Never did I imagine receiving a diagnosis for tongue cancer. I had just responded to God's call for a speaking ministry! My emotions swirled with questions and fears. Talking and swallowing were difficult due to having stitches in my mouth.

Later that evening, I sat at my piano, pouring out my heart to God. Tears flowed as I played hymns, surrendering my questions to him. He took my fears and exchanged them with his deep peace, anchoring me with hope. God's presence became the best refuge for my soul.

Resting in the refuge of God strengthened my body and gave me hope while retraining my tongue to talk. For a while, I said my name as *Nanthy Gwathe*.

Have you ever thought an issue was resolved, only to have it pop up again years later? Eighteen years after the first diagnosis, I thought the cancer was no longer an issue. But then a sore quickly developed on my tongue.

We had moved to a different state and had not yet established medical care. God orchestrated connections within my new church, leading me to an excellent doctor.

At the appointment two days later, he immediately did a biopsy and then scheduled surgery to remove another section of my tongue. I was in God's waiting room again, wondering about my health with a familiar problem.

When fear swelled up in me during the interim time before surgery, God calmed me with Bible verses, bolstering my hope. The doctor removed the cancer. God healed me and deepened my faith.

The refuge of God has been my dwelling place often, as I've had eight tongue biopsies throughout the years with three times being cancerous. Whenever a distressing issue reappears, we can rely on our faithful God. Hope gives us confidence to go forward with God in uncertain times.

I will continue to use my faltering tongue to speak of hope in the best refuge. Now I can say my name correctly. No wonder my heart is glad, and my tongue shouts praises!

Lord, I praise you during the uncertainties of life. Thank you that your hope continually sustains me even when dealing with repeated issues. Help me remember to turn to you at all times. I praise you for being the God of all hope in every situation.

Can You Take a Yoke?

by Beth Kirkpatrick

*Take my yoke upon you. Let me teach you,
because I am humble and gentle at heart, and
you will find rest for your souls.*

MATTHEW 11:29 (NLT)

WHEN YOU CLOSE your eyes to imagine your most treasured place of rest, what do you see? Maybe you envision a flower-filled grassy meadow or a majestic grove of redwood trees with a waterfall splashing beside it. Perhaps your haven is your own front porch, shaded and cool, a quiet library filled with books, or a comfortable bed with crisp sheets and a fluffy duvet.

I feel the most relaxed as I watch the ocean, listening to the waves breaking, breathing in the damp salty air, and timing my breaths to the rhythm of the sea.

I don't imagine carrying a heavy wooden yoke on my shoulders. A yoke sounds the opposite of restful. That sounds like hard work. If I am contemplating rest, I don't want to be carrying anything—I don't even want to be wearing shoes!

But wait a minute. Jesus offers us *his* yoke. What would it be like to be yoked with Jesus? What a privilege to have him beside us every moment of the day, sharing our burdens and joys! We could give up the load of care and guilt the world tries to place on our shoulders alone and learn the humble, gentle ways of our Savior as we walk with him.

If you were prone to straying off the path and wandering the wrong way, you would be yoked to Jesus, and he wouldn't let that happen. You could stop trying to prove that you were the strongest or fastest because the humble and gentle Jesus would be teaching you how to live. You would only have to match your pace and stride to his.

The wonderful news is that all this is possible. Our loving Savior freely offers his grace and mercy to us each day. Jesus wants us to share our cares, woes, hopes, and dreams with him. He knows that our truest rest comes from being in a close relationship with him—more than any physical place to which we can retreat.

Sharing life's ups and downs with Jesus is more refreshing than a barefoot walk on a cool sandy beach.

Dear Jesus, thank you for offering to be yoked with me. Guide my heart with your humility and gentleness. Help me to remember that no matter what is happening around me, my soul can find rest in you.

SNAPSHOTS OF HOPE & HEART

Speaking with Our Ears

by Annie Wolter

For we speak as messengers approved by God
to be entrusted with the Good News.
Our purpose is to please God, not people.
He alone examines the motives of our hearts.

1 Thessalonians 2:4 (NLT)

*L*OOK, ARE YOU going to give me gas money or not?"

"Like I said, I'll gladly come and put gas in your car."

"Just forget it!"

The conversation dissolved in irritation for both parties just as I walked up. I was with a group from church in downtown Madison, Wisconsin, sharing the gospel with anyone who would listen. As my friend walked away, the man and I began to engage. Soon, he was pulling me down the same rabbit hole that frustrated my friend. He kept insisting that the Bible allowed him to get drunk. As I refuted this, I prayed for the right words and felt the Holy Spirit say, "Annie, just listen to him."

"Lord, is that you?" I queried, doubtful. Surely, God wanted me to stand for truth.

But the Lord insisted. "Trust me. Just listen—no matter what he says."

So, I shut my mouth and opened my ears. This challenged me as the guy, Curt, made incorrect statements about God's Word.

Suddenly he stopped and exclaimed, "Hey! You're listening to me, *really* listening!" I chuckled inside and thought of how equally amazed I was at my silence. Our conversation shifted to a tone of camaraderie. We exchanged names and parted on sweet terms. But God wasn't finished with us.

Three weeks later, on a rainy day, God seemed to be leading me to take a bus that was out of the way from my usual line. I doubted but followed, grumpy from the cold. After a few stops, I looked up from my book and got goosebumps. Curt was strolling down the aisle. We were delighted to find each other again! Curt was a war veteran, still finding his bearings. He shared, "I'm on my way downtown for my last unemployment check. Then I'm headed to California for the winter."

As we chatted, I felt God nudging me to give him the book—a small collection of Christian testimonies written for children that I had intended to use with my fifth-grade Sunday school class. I offered it and asked, "Do you think this chance encounter might be from God? Will you read the book?" He did! He would!

The memory of that God-directed moment still gives me joy. God knew what I couldn't possibly know. My new friend needed a listening ear and a compassionate heart. He needed my kindness, not my corrections.

Dear Lord, when you bring opportunities to share the Good News with someone, help me to listen to you. May I be willing to let you direct the encounter—based on the person's needs that only you can see.

Why Can't I Have That?

by Mary Curcio

Incline my heart to your testimonies,
and not to selfish gain.

PSALM 119:36 (ESV)

I LOVED HER, BUT I hated her. She was my mom's favorite child. Why shouldn't she be? She was the baby. Everyone gave her lots of attention, including me. Mom went out of her way to give my sister whatever she wanted. Now that she was no longer a baby, why was my mom still giving her more than she gave me—time, money, attention? I was the oldest child who took care of everyone. Didn't mom realize I also needed her?

While I enjoyed time with my youngest daughter one day, she said, "Mom, I don't know how you did it."

"Did what?" I asked.

"How did you grow up without the kind of good relationship with your mom that you and I have?"

Her comment surprised me. How did she know? I never talked about it. It was "the family secret."

Her remark helped me realize how much I envied how my baby sister was my mom's favorite. I didn't want to be the favorite, but I did want more from Mom. My envy was not only a wedge between my sister and me but between God and me. Being separated from God drove me to his Word.

It was hard, but I had to admit I was selfish. Rather than being thankful for what God had given me, I wanted what my sister had. Knowing my sister was Mom's favorite, I believed I wasn't favored. As I confessed my sin, peace came, and gratitude filled my heart.

While I was praying one day, my baby sister called to let me know that Mom was taking her to Portugal. Instantly I thought, "Why her and not me?" But the Holy Spirit gently reminded me God has given me enough. When she finished talking, I said to her, "Sis, I'm so glad for you. I have never had what you have with Mom, but I'm so glad you do." Those sincere words lifted the wall between us.

Whenever you want something that someone else has, seek God first. He will show you what you *do* have. He knows you can't have everything you want, but he also knows how to fill those painful voids in your life. My daughter's words sent me to God's Word and helped me see how blessed I am. He can do the same for you.

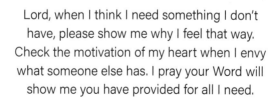

Lord, when I think I need something I don't have, please show me why I feel that way. Check the motivation of my heart when I envy what someone else has. I pray your Word will show me you have provided for all I need.

SNAPSHOTS OF HOPE & HEART

Bridging
the Gap

by Nancy Kay Grace

*And day by day, attending the temple together
and breaking bread in their homes, they received
their food with glad and generous hearts, praising
God and having favor with all the people.*

ACTS 2:46–47 (ESV)

MY HUSBAND, RICK, and I had moved to a new area just prior to the pandemic. One of the challenges of relocation is connecting with a new church family. As I began getting to know people, the pandemic prevented in-person gatherings. The isolation disrupted my connection with our new faith community, creating a gap in making new friends.

During those months, I missed the personal connections at church. When the church re-gathered, the worship and fellowship were much sweeter. I felt joy in seeing a few familiar people. One couple stands out in my mind.

George and Susan chatted with us after a worship service and invited us over for a meal. I visited with Susan while George mingled with others, inviting them as well. I wondered how many people would be at their house. Susan indicated she thought the same thing.

Rick and I arrived at their home before any other guests. We became part of the setup crew, helping bring in chairs from various rooms. George had only a few things remaining to prepare for the meal. Their college-age son eagerly pitched in. Plates were stacked buffet-style on the counter. After counting the number of chairs, Susan smoothed a tablecloth on the long table. Glasses, water pitchers, and silverware were set.

Anticipation buzzed as we prepared for the spur-of-the-moment dinner, which included eight people in addition to the three from the host family.

Their gift of hospitality bridged the gap with fellowship to my faith community. I felt encouraged through the reconnection and even met some new people.

Fellowship is necessary for spiritual growth. I need others to strengthen and encourage my faith, reminding me I am not alone. God created us with a need to connect with others. We are better together.

The early church met together, sharing food, encouragement, and the love of God. Today we can do the same, extending the love of God to those around us through an open table. Perhaps we can bridge the gap for someone else's connection. It all starts by having a generous heart.

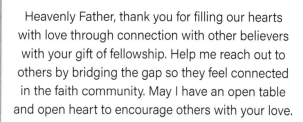

Heavenly Father, thank you for filling our hearts with love through connection with other believers with your gift of fellowship. Help me reach out to others by bridging the gap so they feel connected in the faith community. May I have an open table and open heart to encourage others with your love.

SNAPSHOTS OF HOPE & HEART

Whose Hand Is on the Wheel?

by Mary Harker

The plans of the heart belong to man, but the answer of the tongue is from the LORD.

PROVERBS 16:1 (ESV)

*I*T WAS A typical Wednesday night for my son and me. We were on the way to the midweek programs at our church. Suddenly, our SUV started sliding on invisible ice, and the slickness caused it to seem as if someone else controlled the steering wheel. We swerved into the left lane and avoided hitting the car in front of us. Then the car headed toward a busy cross street. I saw vehicles headed for us out of my peripheral vision. A collision appeared inevitable.

I called out to my son, "Andrew, we are going to crash. Hold on!" By a miracle, we made it across the road without being hit or causing an accident. I'm pretty sure when I get to heaven, I will meet a couple of angels with scars from keeping us safe that night.

Sometimes life is like that night, isn't it? Our day is going as planned, and all is good. Then, the next thing we know, we are sliding out of control, and we feel powerless. Vulnerable and insecure. We don't know how to straighten out of the spin.

In those times, I suggest taking a step back and giving God the wheel. Acknowledge he is in control. God directs our paths, maneuvers our will to line up with his plans, and modifies our destination how he sees best.

The enemy of our soul wants us to think otherwise. Destruction and confusion are his plans for us. To which voice will we listen? The deceiver and liar or our Creator and Savior? By yielding our plans to God's plans, we can have victory. We have a choice between panic and letting God steer our thoughts and actions toward peace.

God is sovereign over all his creation. When an hour, a day, or maybe even a season, seems out of his jurisdiction, take heart. He guides and walks beside us all of our days. And who knows? When life is spinning out of your grasp, you may see your miracle. At the very least, know his hand is on the wheel.

Abba Father, I acknowledge that you are the one who is sovereign over all my days. When I cling to the steering wheel of my life, you are the one who ultimately ordains it all. Help me to rest in your capable hands.

Healing a Broken Heart

by Mary Curcio

A cheerful heart is good medicine, but a broken
spirit saps a person's strength.

PROVERBS 17:22 (NLT)

E WERE EXCITED about the birth of my first grand-son. But it didn't take long to see that something was terribly wrong. So many trips to the emergency room and doctor's office. Doctors performed a battery of tests. No one seemed to know what was wrong—they thought something was wrong with my daughter and me. I was relieved when doctors finally put a name to his condition: Elliot was born with congenital myasthenia gravis. My relief didn't last long as he lay dying in my arms.

My last memory of Elliot is seeing his peaceful face as his body lay in his casket. He hadn't had a peaceful face in a long time. For nine months, we watched him suffer. On one occasion, when he came out of surgery, he couldn't talk, but his face was full of pain. On the day of the funeral, my daughter bent over his casket and kissed the face of her precious son. As she walked away, life would never be the same.

Over the next few months, life felt meaningless. Sleep left me. I couldn't say Elliot's name. Friends and family members moved on with their lives, happy and smiling, while I was stuck in a fog. Didn't they know my grandson died? Doing laundry, going to work, and taking care of my family all became joyless duties. A spirit of heaviness surrounded me while pain became my partner.

As Christmas drew near, my daughter was excited to sing in our church's cantata. She was happy while my heart still ached. The cantata was about the birth of Jesus. How could my daughter, whose son had died, celebrate the birth of God's Son? How could she sing when there were no words to take the pain away? As my daughter smiled and sang praises to God, my pain lifted. My voice joined hers.

God does not abandon us in our pain. He knows how it feels to lose his Son and gain a Savior for the world. From a place of empathy, God brings healing and joy. Observing my daughter overcome her loss by singing praises to a good God gave me hope that sustained me while I waited to heal. "To all who mourn in Israel, he will give a crown of beauty for ashes, a joyous blessing instead of mourning, festive praise instead of despair" (Isaiah 61:3 NLT).

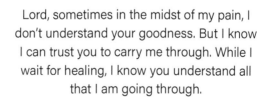

Lord, sometimes in the midst of my pain, I don't understand your goodness. But I know I can trust you to carry me through. While I wait for healing, I know you understand all that I am going through.

SNAPSHOTS OF HOPE & HEART

No Worries, Rudy

by Hally Wells

*Anxiety in a man's heart weighs him down, but a
good word makes him glad.*

PROVERBS 12:25 (ESV)

RUDY, THE REDBONE coonhound—he's the oldest of our
five babies, three of which are human and two of which are
of the canine persuasion. I think on most days, Rudy is my husband's favorite. As we move steadily toward the empty-nest phase,
we enjoy Rudy and his four-legged brother from another mother
more each day.

Redbone coonhounds were bred for hunting, tracking, and
treeing raccoons. They're typically aggressive and fearless in the
field. Our Rudy missed the memo. He's lucky if he can catch the
treats we regularly offer, as we very nearly drop them directly into
the big guy's mouth.

Mine is a blended family, and Rudy is one of my bonus kids,
having been with his single daddy several years before we married.
I'm told he was once a brilliant shade of red, reflective of the
Scottish roots of his breed. Nowadays, Rudy's coat is a sun-dappled
auburn against a background of grey.

At the risk of being indelicate, as redbone Rudy has aged, he's experienced toileting issues. He now wears the latest in dog diapers with a stylish, stretchy-nylon wrap over his paper protection. While some proud pooches might feel emasculated, Rudy remains unperturbed.

Rudy spends most days indoors, gleefully shedding several vacuum cleaner cartridges full of hair each week. Did I mention *his* cleaning routine? More than once during our Wednesday small group Bible study, our precious pup has groomed his private areas with the aggression he's failed to utilize in the forest. That has become his most exhausting workout.

Most would say that Rudy's finest moments are behind him. Some would assert that he may not have much to live for at this point in his life. But what we observe in Rudy is pure contentment and complete joy.

We've got his needs covered. He trusts us wholeheartedly, so he has no reason to fret or worry. We make sure he knows he is loved, so he isn't bothered by his diminished skills, old and unimpressive appearance, unflattering physical problems, or the added burden he places on us.

But Rudy still has things to teach *us*. I know God made us very differently than he made man's best friend, but I think Rudy has figured out how the Creator wants us all to live—trusting without worry that our Father will protect and love us every good, bad, and ugly day of our lives.

Heavenly Father, as I linger in your Word, create in me a spirit of peace and contentment. Help me to trust fully in you, laying my worries down and leaving my burdens with you in prayer.

Test Me, Try Me, Use Me

by Diana Leagh Matthews

Put me on trial, LORD, and cross-examine me.
Test my motives and my heart. For I am always
aware of your unfailing love, and I have lived
according to your truth.

PSALM 26:2–3 (NLT)

*M*Y MOUTH FELL open. A man approached me after leading music at church. "You belong in the ministry."

"No." I took a step back. That's the last thing I expected. Growing up as a preacher's daughter, I knew all the work and heartache that ministry entailed. I had no desire to become a pastor.

Twice more that summer, others repeated the same words, and I continued to rebel against a call to ministry.

By the end of the summer, an argument with a family member inspired me to write my first novel. When I questioned my ability, I heard a whispering in my soul say, *You don't know if you don't try.* I had no idea the long road ahead as I ran from the Lord and his calling on my life.

The following year, I began a downward spiral into an abusive relationship. The only place I had to turn over the next three years was to the Lord. Writing kept me sane, drew me closer to the

Creator, and allowed me the opportunity to discover God's will for my life.

Like David in the Bible, I had to be refined in the fire and tested. I needed a heart exam.

God changed my heart and molded it away from my selfish desires to the plans he had for me. He also revealed there are other types of ministry. For me, it meant writing and music.

The path has not been easy or what I expected. Today's verse inspires me to pray, "Test me, try me, use me, Lord." In doing so, I discover something that makes the journey worth it all—God's unfailing love.

Lord, you know the plans you have for me. Give me a heart to follow you and obey wherever you lead.

A Refreshing Flood

by Darla S. Grieco

I pray that your hearts will be flooded with light so that you can understand the confident hope he has given to those he called—his holy people who are his rich and glorious inheritance.

EPHESIANS 1:18 (NLT)

*T*HE CHURCH VAN rumbled along the backroads of Missouri. My heart sank at seeing only rooftops poking above the flooded farmlands all around us. It was September of '93, and the northeastern regions of the United States had experienced a blizzard in March of that year. Over *four feet* of snow covered the ground in parts of the country.

Then, it melted. Before me lay the aftermath.

Months earlier, the mountains of snow thawed rapidly during the warm spring weeks, forcing the runoff toward the Mississippi River. As a result, the once quaint river rose to a dangerous, tumultuous level. Sleepy towns and innocent bystanders who resided near the river experienced monumental flooding. Lives and livelihoods sat in desperate need of a savior.

When our church missionaries arrived in Missouri six months later to help clean up, we found homes whose windows had not seen the light of day for over six months.

The effects of the flood not only physically washed over their belongings, but the remnants of that flood affected their attitudes and hearts—some, even for a lifetime.

During the event I mentioned, water, which was typically contained within the riverbanks, had risen and drenched the dry land around it. While the word *flood* often carries a negative connotation due to resulting damages, in other cases—like that which comes from the Holy Spirit—it's capable of soaking a parched heart with a fresh anointing.

When Paul wrote to the Ephesians, he desired that Christians' hearts would not just be casually aware of the glorious riches and hope we have in Christ, but that our hearts would be flooded—brimming over the edges, uncontainable and with everlasting effects.

Once we allow God's presence and the truth of his Word to flood all the areas of our lives, our living testimony spills out and becomes a witness to others. Though I'd love to say I've mastered this process, returning to the throne of grace is a constant necessity for me. And as I return to the Lord for more splashing and flooding, his faithfulness reminds me of his ever-present love, renewing the confidence and hope I can only have with him.

> Lord, allow your truths to wash over me. Even when trials come, may I rest like a child in your arms, reassured of your love and faithfulness. And may the life I live out as a result overflow unto others, pointing them to you.

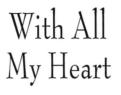

With All
My Heart

by Lori Lipsky

*You will seek me and find me, when you
seek me with all your heart.*

JEREMIAH 29:13 (ESV)

EARS BEFORE OUR daughter was old enough to start school, I worked to help her learn to read. Every day before her naptime, we'd sit together on the sofa. I'd read a tall stack of board books aloud to her. She loved this routine, and so did I.

Before long, she committed entire books to memory. She could "read" them along with me or even on her own. I taught her the sounds of the letters of the alphabet. We played fun word games. As we ran errands, she read letters on store signs. I helped her sound them out. We played at reading all the time.

One day when she was five years old and reading a book, I asked her who had taught her to read. Her answer surprised me. She shrugged and said, "I taught myself."

Her simple response revealed a valuable lesson to me. It's one I'm still learning—one I'll probably be learning for the rest of my life.

In Jeremiah 29:13, the Lord spoke to the exiles in Babylon. He said, "You will seek me and find me, when you seek me with all your heart." We learn here that God wants us to seek after him. But are we completely on our own to make this happen?

Earlier in Jeremiah, God said of the exiles, "I will give them a heart to know that I am the LORD, and they shall be my people and I will be their God, for they shall return to me with their whole heart" (Jeremiah 24:7 ESV). God placed the desire upon their hearts. He equipped them to seek him.

It's the same in this current century. God doesn't leave us to seek him completely on our own strength. His lead comes first, and we follow. Any good thing that comes from us—any good word or action—finds its root in God's work. This includes the act of seeking after him. "For it is God who works in you, both to will and to work for his good pleasure" (Philippians 2:12–13 ESV). Any good thing we say or do first comes from God.

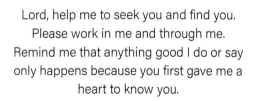

Lord, help me to seek you and find you.
Please work in me and through me.
Remind me that anything good I do or say
only happens because you first gave me a
heart to know you.

On Your Marks!

by Becki James

*Jesus replied, "'You must love
the LORD your God with all your heart,
all your soul, and all your mind.'"*

MATTHEW 22:37 (NLT)

CAN'T DO IT!" As she gasped, her legs buckled, embedding tar and gravel into her knees. Her face throbbed, overloaded with heat—tears streaming into sweat. Dropping further on all fours, she gulped oxygen through dehydrated huffs. For a few seconds, she encapsulated herself in the deafening beat of her heart. *Ta-tump. Ta-tump.* It grew louder and louder until all at once, conscious thought took over, and she recognized the rhythm as feet beating the road around the bend.

Not an ounce of strength remained to move out of the way. Closer. Closer. They would surely trample her. Surging left, her body mashed down the tall grasses in the ditch just as the runners shot by, their feet kicking dust into her eyes and throat.

Defeated, she lay there, coughing and squeezing the dirt from her eyes. Failure replayed in her mind. All she could hear were the heels of those racers stomping over her inept pacing.

But wait.

She abruptly sat up as the hum of real strides heightened.

Who could possibly be lagging this far behind? A numberless shirt rounded the curve, coming into view. The man locked in on her position. Slowing, he halted at her feet. "You missed the checkpoint," he said, extending a hand-up. "Let's finish together, Sis."

⁊

I often feel like that runner—in a marathon of loving God with all my heart, soul, and mind. I start well, giving it all I have. But so often I stagger at the magnitude of the task. How, exactly, do I give all my heart, all my mind, and all my soul? Try as I may, my attempts fall short. I'm weary, running out of steam, and it seems everyone whizzes by me effortlessly. I want to love him with *all my everything*, but I stumble each time I put my foot against the block.

When we set our eyes on our own ability to love God, we lose the race before we begin. But the Holy Spirit is always present to help us in every aspect—even the massive task of loving an infinite God. We are not alone in our journey to love him. We can ask him to help us love him better. The Holy Spirit not only gives us a hand-up, but he is our compass through the hills and turns. If we embrace God's Spirit as our running partner, we win every race before the marks are set.

> Holy Spirit, you know me. You know my weakness, and you know my desire to love you with all my heart, soul, and mind. Remind me to start each moment knowing you are here to help me. Lead me down paths of loving you based on your ever-present love for me.

Broken and Mended

by Stephenie Hovland

"Yet even now," declares the LORD, "return to me with all your heart, with fasting, with weeping, and with mourning; and rend your hearts and not your garments."

JOEL 2:12–13 (ESV)

URING A SPELLING test in my third-grade classroom, a student awkwardly rested her left arm on her desk. As I read aloud each spelling word and sentence, I meandered through the room as usual. The girl didn't even notice that I was soon standing behind her, watching her suspicious behavior.

She lifted her left hand slightly. I saw a spelling word written on her desk. After she copied it onto her paper, I put my hand on her shoulder. She stiffened. Tears followed. I didn't have to say a word. Later that day, the girl was still upset. I pulled her aside to talk about forgiveness and repentance. I'm pretty sure she never tried to cheat on a test again!

When I confess my sins to God, I often feel humility and shame. I could try to justify or avoid it, but nothing can change the fact that I did something contrary to God's commands. I need to confess, "Yes. I did it. Lord, help me." Then I go to the next step—repentance. Repent means to turn away from sin and return to God. That can look different, depending on the person and circumstances. In the Old Testament, it wasn't unusual to have several outward shows of repentance, including offering animal sacrifices and tearing one's clothing.

God cares more about what's happening on the inside than the outside. Public confession is fine, but if our hearts are not in it, then it isn't real. It's just a show. When we rend, or tear apart, our hearts, it means we feel, know, and live that repentance. We mean what we say, and we live the change. Often, that change is difficult, so it does feel as if something inside us is torn up.

Thank God, he gives us the solution. He doesn't tell us to rely on ourselves and find our inner confidence. No, God gives us special healing for torn-up hearts. He sends the Holy Spirit to comfort us with his message of grace through his Son. The Spirit indwells and strengthens us through the power of repentance and with change only he can bring. Through this spiritual healing, our hearts are mended.

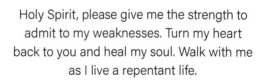

Holy Spirit, please give me the strength to admit to my weaknesses. Turn my heart back to you and heal my soul. Walk with me as I live a repentant life.

SNAPSHOTS OF HOPE & HEART

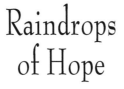

Raindrops of Hope

by TLC Nielsen

*My soul longs, yes, faints for the courts
of the LORD; my heart and flesh sing
for joy to the living God.*

PSALM 84:2 (ESV)

I WANDERED AROUND THE church grounds, the cloudy day matching my mood. This particular winter had been tough, so I carved out a day to spend with God—outside. When the rain picked up, I decided to seek shelter but stopped when sunlight suddenly peeked through. Droplets hung off evergreen branches, glittering like diamonds.

I pulled out my phone to capture the beauty of the moment, but as I examined the pine trees up close, I noticed red tips of new cones forming—a drop of water dangling from each one. I reached out to touch a cone. A raindrop clung to my finger. I held the droplet, turning my hand over to see if it would stay. It did.

I sat under a tree, savoring the moment God provided. How often does one hold a raindrop? The birdcalls in the rain surrounded me as I watched small birds enjoy the empty sky, no bigger ones in sight. Oh, how the leaves and branches quivered in the earth-scented breeze. My world—gray and wintry—blossomed in God's presence, the colors of spring filling my soul.

Tears and rain intermixed as my heart filled with joy. I thanked the Lord for his love, his creation, his attention to detail.

Humming to myself, I stood and wondered what else God wanted to show me. Eagerly, I strode along the roadside. He whispered, "Slow down, you're missing it." I stopped and looked around. Kneeling, I peered at the stones and new green grass. A tiny pink flower nestled close to the ground. Once I noticed it, I saw intermittent flashes of pink scattered across the area. I took that moment to praise him for the beauty I almost missed.

The rest of my day continued like this as I slowly walked at God's pace seeing the amazing handiwork he created, even rain bubbles popping in a pond. The grayness of my hurried life evaporated as I learned to relax and carry a raindrop of hope—his hope—within my heart.

His lesson stays with me, and I now take a day of rest, relaxation, and prayer every week where I savor each bite of food and see with his eyes again.

God uses quiet moments to remind us in our hurriedness to slow down and rest in his goodness. After all, even *he* rested after creating the world and made that day holy.

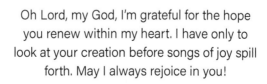

Oh Lord, my God, I'm grateful for the hope you renew within my heart. I have only to look at your creation before songs of joy spill forth. May I always rejoice in you!

Wisdom in Every Generation

by Edna Earney

My child, if your heart is wise, my own heart
will rejoice! Everything in me will celebrate when
you speak what is right.

PROVERBS 23:15–16 (NLT)

"I F I TRY to do *all* the good things, they can become bad things," said our eldest granddaughter, Madelyn. She had decisions to make, and she was learning to prioritize. As a sophomore nursing student, should she take the leadership role offered by a Christian club on campus? Accept the position of resident assistant for her dorm? Try out for drill team? Take a summer class or an extra class in the fall?

Our lunchtime with her family was passing quickly. Everyone weighed in about her choices, and I bit my lip to keep from urging her toward my preferences. "Which of these would you hate to miss out on?" I asked, with a hint of "seize the day" in my tone.

She answered, "These are all good things to do. But I don't want to be average at three jobs. I want to be good at two. And college classes come first."

I smiled, and a happy tear glistened as I took in the wisdom of her statement. I stopped to write down her words, literally grabbing a nearby envelope and pencil, knowing I would quote her in the future. This eighteen-year-old spoke wisdom some adults have not learned, and I was her grateful gammie.

People often refer to each position of responsibility as a hat we wear, so being a wife, mother, and teacher equals three hats. One psychologist said most people manage two and one-half full-time hats well. Juggling three hats or more causes stress and lower productivity. Madelyn's choice to accept only two hats spoke well of her priorities and how thoughtfully she'd considered her schedule.

We can identify with Solomon in Proverbs and his effort to pass wisdom to his son. Expecting his son would want to please him, Solomon doesn't stop at saying, "Gain wisdom." He adds that seeing the fruit of wisdom, his son speaking "what is right" would make everything in him celebrate. We want the next generation to learn from us, and we delight in acknowledging their good choices.

That delight leads friends to smile at our social media posts about proud parent or grandparent moments: the birth of a child, making a team, holiday gatherings. But we agree with Solomon that "if your heart is wise, my own heart will rejoice!" We applaud loudest when we view God's handiwork in a child's heart through an outward demonstration of inner wisdom.

Dear Father, thank you for confirming the mother's heart within me that rejoices when I see wisdom in my children and grandchildren. Please give me insight when I have my own decisions to make. I want to do and speak what is right to help others see you and your wisdom.

#GodIsGood

by Teresa Janzen

*I will praise you, LORD, with all my heart; I will
tell of all the marvelous things you have done.*

PSALM 9:1 (NLT)

*H*AVE YOU EVER had a nostalgic memory pop up in your
social media newsfeed? We share milestones, accomplishments, and glimpses into everyday life with incredible ease. Today's
post of a special event, funny moment, or new experience may
come back later as a memory to warm your heart once again.

When I scroll through my memories with God, I find
encouragement, joy, humility, and renewed faith. I remember the
conversation with a loved one where ministering words flowed
effortlessly and brought comfort. A harrowing car ride that nearly
ended in tragedy still makes my heart race. Then there was the
time I prayed with a child as she asked Jesus into her heart. Each
memory fills my heart with awe and praise and reminds me of
God's love for me as he draws me closer.

Reflecting on God's goodness strengthens my heart, and sharing his good deeds points others toward Christ. Jesus said, "Let your good deeds shine out for all to see, so that everyone will praise your heavenly Father" (Matthew 5:16 NLT). The most effective way I can share God's goodness with others is to tell them what he has done in my life. This is my testimony, and no one can argue with my personal experience.

Reflecting on the marvelous things God has done fills our hearts and spills over in a way sure to be noticed by others. Sometimes we think we need to be a theologian to share with someone about God, but all we really need to do is tell them what he has done for us. The joy and gratitude that fuel our testimony become a shining beacon drawing people to experience God for themselves.

Marvelous God, I praise you for all you have done for me. You have accepted me as your own and invited me to share your love with others. Help me declare your good deeds in a way that draws people to you.

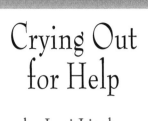

Crying Out for Help

by Lori Lipsky

I pray with all my heart; answer me, LORD!
I will obey your decrees.

PSALM 119:145 (NLT)

*H*AVE YOU EVER cried out to the Lord for help? During the recent pandemic, the pressures and stresses of life weighed on my heart, and I experienced difficulties sleeping. I often awakened during the middle of the night with thoughts spinning. My mind dwelled on my concerns, and I succumbed to worry.

But sometimes, I remembered to look to the Lord. I prayed for help, or I listened to the Bible through an app on my phone, using headphones in order to keep from waking the others in my house.

In the psalms, we read examples of God's people calling out to him for help. The ending of Psalm 119:145 used to seem ill-fitting to me. I wondered why the words "I will obey your decrees" were included.

In the passage, the psalmist pleaded to God from the depths of his heart. Not only that, but he also asked for strength and help to obey God. His cries for help mingled with cries that he would obey the commands of the Lord. Likewise, when our prayers to the Lord are aligned with an obedient heart, powerful things happen.

When I ran across Proverbs 28:9, I better understood. "God detests the prayers of a person who ignores the law" (NLT). When we tell the Lord we desire to obey him as we plead for his help, we are praying as the psalmist did.

Our prayers don't need to be elegant or long or well-articulated. If we're calling to him from an honest heart and desiring to be obedient to the truth we find in the Scriptures, we're on the right track.

Lord, when I am in trouble or distress, remind me to call out to you. I desire to have a compliant heart behind my prayers. I confess that I often fall short, but nonetheless, you are my refuge. You are my fortress and deliverer. Thank you for your Word.

Wholehearted

by Robin Steinweg

*O my son, give me your heart. May your eyes
take delight in following my ways.*

PROVERBS 23:26 (NLT)

*D*O YOU KNOW a daydreamer? Someone who is absent-minded, preoccupied, and scatterbrained—like a puppy in a field of bones. The puppy grabs a bone, sees another, drops the first, sees several more, and oh my, all that goodness! Which way to turn?

I've lived in that field of bones all my life. I've searched out methods to thwart this tendency to go every direction at once. If I were a horse, I'm sure I'd be given blinders. For myself, in a worship service, I sit near the front. While at work, I wear sound-canceling headphones to silence barking dogs. In conversations, I intentionally focus my eyes and ears on the person speaking.

Maybe everyone deals with distraction to some extent. When my sons were growing up, if I wanted them to really hear my words, I'd gently take their face in both hands and get their undivided attention before I spoke. They did the same to me when they wanted *my* attention.

And then there is God's desire for my single-minded attention. Considering that there's no voice I'd rather hear than his, no counsel, correction, or comfort I'd rather receive than his, how is it possible that my attention—my heart—could be so wayward? Why would my eyes want to look anywhere else than to his beauty, forgiveness, kindness, and love?

In Proverbs, Solomon was talking to his son, encouraging him in ways that lead to wisdom. But we can deduce that these same principles work between our heavenly Father and his children. In Psalm 86:11, the writer asked for an undivided heart to honor God. I can sure agree with that.

The Bible says God is a jealous God. It even says his very name is Jealous (see Exodus 34:14). He wants my heart! Even when my attention wanders, even when I myself wander, he loves me and wants me. Jesus's human heart actually stopped beating in order to make the way for my heart to be his.

When I've responded to him with faith and become his own, then he wants me to fix my eyes on him. He takes my face in his hands and says, "Observe me closely. Delight in my ways and follow me."

God wants me to be all his. Wholehearted.

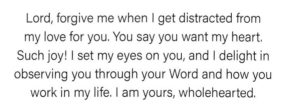

Lord, forgive me when I get distracted from my love for you. You say you want my heart. Such joy! I set my eyes on you, and I delight in observing you through your Word and how you work in my life. I am yours, wholehearted.

Ready for Anything

by Stephenie Hovland

*He is not afraid of bad news; his heart is
firm, trusting in the LORD.*

PSALM 112:7 (ESV)

A S A FOURTH grader, I used the school bathroom stalls to practice different ways I might have to use the bathroom in the future. What would it be like if I were blind? If I couldn't use my right arm? If my left foot were missing? I also mentally rehearsed what I would do if my bus crashed at any point on our ride home.

One day, our bus slid off an icy road, and I got to practice the scenario "What would you do if you're stranded on the bus in the snow and really had to pee?" It was the ultimate combination of my worst-case scenarios. Thank goodness I had trained!

Instead of looking forward to the future because of reasonable preparation, I kept waiting for the next bad thing to happen. I lived in a state of discontent.

Recently I have come to terms with the side of me that wants survival skills (that's good!) and the side of me that wants to worry about every worst-case scenario (not good). The Holy Spirit works in me to help me focus on being thankful for what I have and leaving the future to him. Through Bible reading and prayer, I experience more joy and peace. God helps me focus on the good things and dream (a little less) of the possible nightmares.

Last week, a loved one said he was having some concerning physical symptoms and should see his doctor soon. As I walked away, I prayed, "God, I'm ready for the next big thing. Because you're already there."

Within ten minutes, I was transporting that man to the ER, where we spent most of the day. I didn't despair or fear. I was able to ease his mind with my calm presence, crack jokes with him, and drive a little faster than I usually do because God was there, and I knew it. (He's okay, by the way. You weren't imagining the worst-case scenario, were you?)

I still like to practice some survival skills, but I don't need to constantly imagine the worst. God encourages me to appreciate today as he strengthens me for the future. My hope depends on God's plans, not mine.

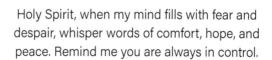

Holy Spirit, when my mind fills with fear and despair, whisper words of comfort, hope, and peace. Remind me you are always in control.

Laundry
Room Woes

by Hally Wells

Love the LORD your God, walk in all his ways,
obey his commands, hold firmly to him, and
serve him with all your heart and all your soul.

JOSHUA 22:5 (NLT)

EW POTENTIAL PURCHASES are exciting enough to get me into stores on Christmas Eve. Actually, I'd prefer not to shop anytime for anything. I'm low maintenance like that. Nevertheless, when your washing machine takes its last spin around the laundry room, and you're facing two weeks with two young adults at home and loads—lots of them—of dirty laundry, what is a low-maintenance momma to do?

My husband and I ventured out to our preferred big-box store. If only we could find a salesperson! I think most were hiding out from last-minute customers or gearing up for fun before clocking out.

After we finally found someone to help us, we outlined our washer requirements. Something highly efficient. Two adult kids are costly enough without spending extra dollars on electricity, water, and detergent. Does it occur to any that the words "low-maintenance momma" are as simpatico as the words "adult kids" are an oxymoron?

With our family's clean clothes criteria in mind, we considered the impeller-versus-agitator debate. We chose impeller. Fancy wasn't a priority, but we wanted a model that could hold more than our last one. Our children, not concerned with a long-lasting appliance *or* garments, had begun washing entire wardrobes together—creating bigger loads. They were all about preserving *their* energy rather than the washer's! It needed to handle the weight of extra-large loads without breaking the bank. A machine that would do its thing diligently, without problems or needed repairs. That isn't too much to ask, is it?

I have to ponder—perhaps cleanliness *is* next to godliness. While our heavenly Father does not see us as machines or robots, his expectations of us may be similar to those I have for my favorite household appliance.

Almighty God desires followers who wholeheartedly use the gifts and talents they've been given to serve him. God calls upon believers to meet the needs of others. He wants us to do our best, rather than the bare minimum, each day. Moreover, he directs us to work for him without faltering, though he understands we are human rather than machine, and he knows we will fail, flounder, and fall short along the way.

What an honor it is to be invited to serve God every day. I'm glad for the printed instructions he gives in the Bible to serve him with all my heart. So much better than the guide that came with my new washing machine!

Gracious God, thank you for equipping me to be a servant in your kingdom. Help me to serve with all my heart and soul. May I joyfully and tirelessly use the gifts you gave me in order to spread your Word and minister to your children.

Faithful Heart, Stable Home

by Charlaine Martin

*Never let loyalty and kindness leave you! Tie them
around your neck as a reminder. Write them deep
within your heart. Then you will find favor with both
God and people, and you will earn a good reputation.*

PROVERBS 3:3–4 (NLT)

*Y*ELLING PUNCTUATED BY shattering glass still haunts me. Only four years old, I snuck down the stairs to check out the noise and cautiously peek around the doorway. Dad's coffee table glass lay broken in tiny pieces along with his coffee mug. "You're *insane*!" they shouted at each other as hot tempers flared. Eventually, Mom and Dad divorced. My mother remarried only to endure a battered ending for that marriage too. While growing up, my heart was broken from violence and caustic words.

I determined to have a better marriage but could have easily repeated this devastating lifestyle. It was all I knew, yet God had a plan. He led me to meet a young Christian man whose parents exemplified a healthy marriage. What a refreshing difference! I wanted that kind of home for my family.

I learned patience in my first marriage, which required a double dose of forgiveness and kindness—essential ingredients for a healthy marriage. Patience withstands many storms, and kindness takes the bite out of an argument. Forgiveness heals the heart. Those horrible memories from my past never crept into our relationship, and God blessed us.

Years later, cancer took his life. At the funeral, several visitors exclaimed how our marriage testified of our faithful love. Their generous praise surprised me. The testimony of a Christ-centered marriage speaks volumes without saying a word.

When I met my second husband, he recognized the love-filled stability he desired. If my childhood dictated the fate of this marriage, we would have already crashed. Divorce isn't an option for us since we trust God's Word about marriage. My late husband's example of a faithful love influences my midlife remarriage today. My husband's family noticed these qualities blossom in our marriage and happily told me so.

Loyalty and kindness are rare qualities in marriage today. Marriage takes devoted time and energy to nurture and grow. Arguments aren't bad. In fact, they can bring about valuable changes.

No marriage is perfect, but it has the possibility of shining as a beacon of hope. Regardless of your past, you can establish a lifelong marriage by practicing patience, forgiveness, and kindness. Imitate God's faithfulness. Not only will people remember it, but they might also imitate *you*. Your marriage can be a testimony of Christ living through you. What a good reputation!

Dear God, thank you for the influence of others who set the example of what a healthy, faithful marriage can be. Please help me be patient and kind to my husband, even when I don't feel like it. Help me resist the temptation to run away or lash out when we go through difficult times. May your Word and your love be ever-present in our home.

Perfect Love

by Mindy Cantrell

*May the Lord make your love for one another
and for all people grow and overflow, just as our
love for you overflows. May he, as a result, make
your hearts strong, blameless, and holy.*

1 THESSALONIANS 3:12–13 (NLT)

I HAVE A LADY in my life who I love very much—now. There were many years when I didn't. You see, she took something precious of mine and kept it from me. Her actions devastated me and destroyed my love for her. After years of harboring this pain in my heart, I finally made the difficult choice to forgive her.

One day, while reciting the Lord's prayer, God stopped me. As I asked him to help me forgive without holding grudges toward those who had sinned against me, he whispered her name upon my heart. I felt him ask, "What about her?"

I responded, "But God, I *have* forgiven her."

I sensed God reply, "Beloved, is there a bitter spot here in your heart when you think of her?" He knows me so well.

Even though I had forgiven this lady, I realized a part of me still felt bitterness toward her. This little piece of bitterness I clung to held my feelings captive and affected my relationship with her family. My heart hurt to know I held this bitterness within me. I immediately asked God to forgive me, to pull that bitter root out, and replace it with his perfect love for her. From that day forward, my affection for my friend began to grow once more.

Is there someone in your life you find difficult to love? Maybe they're bossy or egocentric. Maybe they are too perfect. Maybe they've done something to hurt you. Perhaps it's even yourself you're finding it hard to love. Don't worry, you are not alone.

In our own strength, our love is usually conditional and swayed by our positive or negative life experiences. However, when we ask God to fill us with *his* love for another, then it's *his* perfect, enduring love that we feel instead of our own frail and faulty emotions. A heart filled with God's love, not only for ourselves but for all humanity, produces a strong and vibrant heart. Strong because it draws from God's love to care for others.

This is how we allow God to make our love for one another grow and overflow. When our love is growing and overflowing with God's love, our hearts become strong, blameless, and holy.

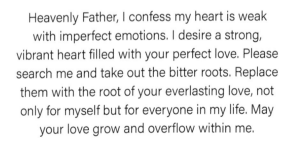

Heavenly Father, I confess my heart is weak with imperfect emotions. I desire a strong, vibrant heart filled with your perfect love. Please search me and take out the bitter roots. Replace them with the root of your everlasting love, not only for myself but for everyone in my life. May your love grow and overflow within me.

SNAPSHOTS OF HOPE & HEART

Hitting a
New Low

by Nancy Graves

O LORD, *do good to those who are good, whose*
hearts are in tune with you.

PSALM 125:4 (NLT)

MY VOICE CRACKED again, and I groaned in frustration. *I'm never going to hit that note!*

Father's Day was a week away, and I was the slated soloist. I'd chosen a song that was not only well-suited for the occasion, but it was also beautiful. I looked forward to performing it, but even more, I couldn't wait to share it with the congregation. I knew it would be a blessing.

Practicing often, I tried to sing the whole song through smoothly. But each time, I stumbled. There was a low note I couldn't get my larynx around. I did my best to make it work by staying hydrated, warming up my vocal cords, preparing my muscle memory, and even not drinking milk.

But as the day drew near, every run toward that section still ended on a gravelly note—out of tune and far from pleasant. I had to admit, no matter how hard I tried, that note was beyond my reach. It was never going to sound like I wanted. But the thought of shelving the song made me sad. I had such a sense of peace when I chose it. It seemed to be God's pick. Now, I had no peace.

I shared my dilemma with a fellow choir member, and she had a good idea. Her husband was a tenor. She would ask him if he was willing to take my place on Sunday—and sing that song. He agreed.

As much as I wanted to sing it, I wouldn't trade places with him for the world! The song was well within his vocal range—each note perfectly in tune. His voice was warm and smooth—his delivery, heartfelt and flawless. The performance resonated with everyone long after the service was over. It was a good thing I couldn't hit that low note. It needed someone new who could do it justice.

I realized that both of us *were* in tune—with God. He led me to pick the right song and led my friend's husband to sing it. We were in the sweet spot of God's goodness, blessed to do our part in his blessing to the congregation.

Have you lost your peace? Look to God. Limitations become invitations to see him at work. When our hearts are in tune with him, he leads us into the sweet spot of his goodness.

Dear God, you alone are good. Thank you for the blessing of your goodness in my life. Please help me look to you each day to keep my heart in tune with yours, so my life can display your goodness to others.

Friends of
the Heart

by Lori Lipsky

*Pursue righteous living, faithfulness, love, and
peace. Enjoy the companionship of those who call
on the Lord with pure hearts.*

2 Timothy 2:22 (nlt)

*T*HREE YEARS INTO our marriage, my husband and I sat
together on our sofa for an important conversation. Several
messages at church had challenged us to grow in our relationship
with the Lord. We were fairly young in our faith at the time. We
both desired to live more godly lives, but we had a long way to go.

Though we had a lot to learn, we weren't sure how to proceed.
Maybe others knew. We'd learned what a strong influence those
you spend time with can have, so we came to a conclusion. We decided to be more deliberate about choosing friends.

At the time, we attended church on Sundays and were part
of a weekly Bible study, but we weren't inviting friends over much.
The church we attended happened to include a large population of
young couples. If our plan was to get more serious about our faith,
we wondered who we could learn from. Who might encourage us
and show us the way? We made a list of three couples we respected
and admired and decided to invite them over one at a time.

That week, we hosted one of the couples for dinner and games. They brought their young children along, and we had a wonderful time. One year later, all three couples were among our closest friends. We loved the opportunity to engage in dialogue with believers who walked further ahead in their spiritual journey. What a blessing to rub elbows with them.

The Scriptures instruct us to pursue righteous living, love, and peace. We're to pray we might live a peaceful, quiet life. And we're encouraged to enjoy the companionship of others who call on the name of the Lord. What a blessing.

Lord, I ask you to allow me to live a quiet life of godliness and dignity. Please guide and direct who I spend time with. Thank you for the wonderful privilege of associating with others who call on your name.

Letting God Work

by Charlaine Martin

Trust in the LORD with all your heart; do not depend on your own understanding. Seek his will in all you do, and he will show you which path to take.

PROVERBS 3:5–6 (NLT)

J ANSWERED THE PHONE and heard, "Mom. I left my husband. We are safe at a domestic violence shelter." My heart leaped out of my chest! In despair, I sank into my hospital bed, where I was recovering from a heart attack just two days before. I felt helpless to do anything for Paige,* who lived clear across the country. Everything in me screamed, *Help your daughter and grandkids!* I wanted to hop on a plane and bring them home, but I couldn't.

Tearfully, I told my husband about her call. He sat by my bedside, "Honey, you can't do anything for her right now. Let's pray." So, he took my hands, and we prayed fervently. I yearned to help, but doing so could cause serious legal issues for my daughter. I realized Paige had to go through the proper channels where she lived. As soon I could travel, I went to help them.

God intervened for them over and over, providing protection and resources. He brought a Christian woman to take her and the children to safety when a Colorado microburst-turned-hailstorm put them in danger while waiting for a bus. The same woman helped her get a job to support her family. Countless times, God showed up through strangers who became friends, and she recognized his miraculous work in their lives.

While eating dinner after a special event, I was recently blessed to meet some people whom God sent to care for my daughter and her kids in my place. These sweet souls shared stories of how God used them in her family's life. All I could do was praise God and thank him for being Paige's rescuer and provider.

Sometimes, what we think we should do isn't in God's plans. We may need to step aside in prayer, watching for opportunities to do what God reveals to us. It may be utterly nothing until he points us in the right direction. Watching with anticipation challenges us when it comes to our loved ones. We can trust God is at work ahead of us and give him glory for the outcome.

Do you feel helpless in the circumstances of a family member or friend? Trust that God loves them more than you do. Pray for his protection, guidance, and intervention. Watch expectantly for his loving hope in ways that will blow away your imagination. Then share God's love-filled hope with those involved.

*Name changed

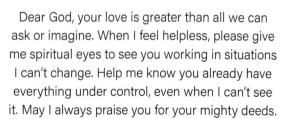

Dear God, your love is greater than all we can ask or imagine. When I feel helpless, please give me spiritual eyes to see you working in situations I can't change. Help me know you already have everything under control, even when I can't see it. May I always praise you for your mighty deeds. Thank you for hope beyond all measure.

All In

by Sally Ferguson

*And you must love the LORD your God with all
your heart, all your soul, and all your strength.*

DEUTERONOMY 6:5 (NLT)

S PLASH! THE BUOYANCY of the waves rocked across the
pool and splattered my sun-kissed skin. I smiled as the
toddler's mom scooped her up securely in a wet embrace. How
many parents over the annals of time had reenacted this familiar
ritual? The giggling toddler wriggled out of her mother's arms to
repeat the process—no coaching necessary. That child was all in.

I thought of all of the times my own two had trusted me to
catch them as they emerged into their teens and adult years. We
jumped into life's whirlpools, gulping for air, and splashed with joy
in life's victories. I never questioned my determination to be available to my offspring. I wanted to be there. Even when my methods
were faulty, I was all in for my family.

I reminisced about my three grands and the unbridled delight
on their faces. There are no limits to what I would do for them.
I'm inspired by how they love wholeheartedly with such innocence
and purity. Their love is all in for Gra'ma, who adores them.

I reflected on my Abba, Daddy. The Lord patiently wades into the pool of life with me. He is a strong arm when I am in over my head and a secure lighthouse when the storms slap against my esteem. His track record for being faithful to his children is a testimony for those who seek him. All the time, he is all in for me.

What can I offer to the One so gracious to me? I have nothing to give but that which he has already given me. I offer him my all—my emotions, my essence, and my endurance. My hope is to bring praise to his name through the glory of his faithfulness.

Lord, I am all in. My heart is full of love for you. I commit to following your ways and trusting your heart. Thank you for your faithfulness. May my life be an example of jumping all in to follow you.

Sniffles, Coughs, and Sneezes

by Dorothy Mae Spradley

"I am leaving you with a gift—peace of mind and heart. And the peace I give is a gift the world cannot give. So don't be troubled or afraid."

JOHN 14:27 (NLT)

*H*ER VOICE BROKE with sniffles, coughs, and sneezes as the Negro spiritual she sang filled the convenience store. For a moment, I almost forgot where I was. Broom in hand, surrounded by co-workers and customers, she sang about being changed and knowing it.

When it was my turn at the register, I should have thanked her for such a gift. What came out was, "Girl, my allergies are messing me up too."

To which she replied, "I know. These allergies are messing us all up."

I don't know if you're like me, but I tend to get frustrated with the sniffles, coughs, and sneezes of life. I want exemption from any and all pain, but there's no such thing. A Christian who avoids pain displays a lack of trust in God's ability to carry us through life's obstacles.

But something significant happens within a person when Christ becomes their source of peace. By spending time with Jesus daily, we cultivate this peace that he is so eager to give. More and more, even in hardships, our minds and our hearts grow undisturbed and confident in him. Secure in Christ, he strengthens us as we endure life and flourish through whatever he allows to impact us. With a quiet, untroubled spirit, we face life's challenges unafraid.

By way of this gift of peace, as God allows, insecurities and self-consciousness disappear. Convenience stores transform into sanctuaries. Sweeping up offers praise to God. Like our store clerk, we become unashamed of the change he's made in our lives and capable of displaying confidence in Christ no matter what and no matter where.

Jesus, what a gift of peace you've given me. Thank you for planting it in my heart. Help me recognize that no matter what, you are always with me. May I confidently display how I trust you, regardless of where I am.

Rescued
by Love

by Lisa-Anne Wooldridge

*But I have trusted in your steadfast love; my
heart shall rejoice in your salvation. I will sing to
the LORD, because he has dealt bountifully with me.*

PSALM 13:5–6 (ESV)

I JUMPED OUT OF our still-moving minivan and snatched up
the little girl from the middle of the street. She couldn't have
been more than two years old. She clung to me and wasn't about
to let go. My husband finished parking the car as I carried her to
the sidewalk and toward the busy farmer's market we were about
to visit.

A man stepped up to me and tried to take her out of my arms,
thanking me for my quick action. But she held on to me, and my
first instinct was to turn away from this man and look for someone
else. He persisted, but a still small voice inside of me insisted I
not let her go. He walked beside me for a block, trying to reason
with me and cajole me into letting him have her, but I just kept
walking.

Then I saw her. It was clear who the parent of this child
was—a look of sick terror covered her face. I could see her lips
moving as she prayed, "Please God, my baby!"

As I moved toward her, the man beside me melted away into the crowd and disappeared. He had herded the little girl away from her mother in the crowd, and she, lost and afraid, had run into the street where I found her. The child jumped from my arms to her mother. I was so thankful. God had rescued her and let me help.

Once again, God proved himself mighty to save. You see, I was also abducted as a toddler. My parents lived on base in the Army, and a discharged soldier and his wife who lived next door were moving out. They took me from my bouncy seat on the porch and drove away with me in the cab of their truck. A young soldier manning the exit gate had held them up for strange behavior when the call came through to look out for a missing child. His God-given instinct helped save me.

When I think about the steadfast, saving love of God over so many areas of my life, I cling to him even tighter. I recognize who I can trust. I know who will save me, deliver me, and deal bountifully with me. I sing to my rescuer and put all my hope in him.

Thank you, Father, for your constant care and for freeing me from every danger and trap. Thank you for rescuing me and leading me safely home. I rejoice in your salvation, and I rest in your steadfast love!

Our
Contributors

KRISTINE ACCOLA is a glass-half-full kinda gal. A writer and animal lover, she holds fast to her belief in Jesus Christ. With grit, humor, and a pioneer spirit, Kris believes the joy is in the journey, and the adventure is wherever you are. Published in *Wit, Whimsy & Wisdom*, she also supports other writers by collaborating on their book projects. Shoot her an email at misskay.accola@gmail.com. She'd love to visit with you!

DENISE MARGARET ACKERMAN shares her passion for God as she sings with a worship team and leads Bible studies. As a contributing author to her church newsletter, Denise encourages readers to wholeheartedly follow the Lord. She has been married for forty-seven years to James, aka "Mr. Adventure." With eight grandchildren, they enjoy riding four-wheelers and making s'mores at their Upstate New York farm cabin. You can reach her at dackerman.0922@gmail.com.

EVA BURKHOLDER'S experience as a missionary kid, cross-cultural worker, and member care provider adds a global dimension to her study of Scripture and storytelling. Through her blog (www.evaburkholder.com) and her book, *Favored, Blessed, Pierced: A Fresh Look at Mary of Nazareth*, Eva invites readers to slow down, reflect, and apply God's Word. She and her husband live in Texas and enjoy spending time with their two sons and daughter-in-law.

The heartbeat of **MINDY CANTRELL'S** life is sharing a little hope and a lot of grace with every soul she meets. Drawing from personal experience, she passionately leads her ladies' groups to and through God's healing love for their lives. She and husband Bill reside in Texas, Facetiming avidly with their daughter, son-in-law, and long-awaited granddaughter. Mindy is also published in the WordGirls collective *Wit, Whimsy & Wisdom*. Learn more about Mindy at www.mindycantrell.com.

Award-winning author **MARY CURCIO** desires to help women overcome adverse circumstances and leave a "God legacy." She may be retired as a school administrator after twenty-five years in education, but you can still find her teaching Bible studies and Sunday school. Mary serves her community and as the women's ministry leader in her church. With fourteen grandchildren, her heart is full. Find Mary on Facebook @mary.o.curcio.

NATASHA LYNN DANIELS is a Christian communicator, author, and the founder of Faithful Hope Ministries. Her purpose is to encourage women to seek joy, live by faith, and hold on to hope. Her words inspire believers to suffer strong for Jesus so they can be filled with the hope and joy of the Lord even when it seems impossible. Natasha's favorite titles are wife and mom. www.natashalynndaniels.com.

EDNA EARNEY revels in blooming rosebuds, diamonds uncovered from coal, and life-renewing literature for their transformational moments. She taps into those truth-filled times so her readers see their own hard days can sculpt potential treasures. Together with her husband, Mike, Edna enjoys sharing God's good news for relationships as a Prepare-Enrich marriage mentor and trainer. Retired from teaching English, she has contributed to several compilations, including *Wit, Whimsy & Wisdom*. Contact Edna on Facebook @TapIntoTransformation.

SALLY FERGUSON loves to dive into God's Word and splash his refreshing water onto others. She speaks and writes with a look at snapshots of life in the sunshine and in the storms. Sally plans women's retreats, and she's working on a Bible study for caregivers. She lives in the beautiful countryside of Jamestown, New York, with her husband and her dad. Visit Sally's blog at www.sallyferguson.net.

NANCY KAY GRACE offers the hope of grace to those she meets. As a cancer survivor, she understands dealing with unexpected challenges. Because life is unedited—or not perfect—we need God's grace. She is an engaging Bible teacher, speaker, and award-winning author of the devotional *The Grace Impact*. Nancy is married to her favorite pastor. She loves hugs from grandchildren, playing piano, and hiking. Nancy's blog and *GraceNotes* newsletter signup are found at www.nancykaygrace.com.

NANCY GRAVES offers hope, encouragement, and a smile along the way. A storyteller at heart, she shares her life experiences with candor and sincerity. Providing personal insight—all from a biblical perspective—she delves into various topics from life's trials and marriage issues to contentment and spiritual growth. A multi-published author, she has contributed to four women's devotional books, blog posts, and other publications. She also offers editorial services. Nancy can be reached at nleegraves@gmail.com.

DARLA S. GRIECO is a keyboard-tapping gal who loves to fellowship with others about personal growth and faith. In 2014, Darla stepped out of her comfort zone to pursue her dream of becoming a writer. Since then, her short stories and devotionals have appeared in various publications. When she isn't at her laptop, Darla can be found enjoying family, playing tennis, or marveling at God's glorious creation. She'd love for you to visit her at www.dsgrieco.com.

Following in the footsteps of Florence Nightingale, **MARY HARKER,** a former nurse, aims to use the lamp of God's Word to shine light into a dark world. Her desire is to illuminate the path and guide readers in the truth, freedom, hope, and power of Jesus. A contributing author to *Wit, Whimsy & Wisdom* and chrisitiandevotions.us, Mary resides with her people near Rockford, Illinois. Connect with her at harker.mary96@gmail.com or Facebook and Instagram.

KELLY HERR, MEd, shares her life experiences to encourage others. An overcomer, Kelly knows the persistent love of her Savior and desires to bring light to the darkness in life's hardest battles. A sports coach for many years, her message is always the same—"Never give up." Kelly is an elementary principal and loves to play pickleball. You can connect with her on Facebook at "Learning to fly with broken wings" @kellyherrauthor.

STEPHENIE HOVLAND wants to help others connect to God. She finds unique ways each of us can kindle the fires of our faith-filled lives. As a pastor's wife, former teacher, and mother of two grown girls, she's the first to admit she has plenty to work on. Join Stephenie as she walks alongside other Christian women, sharing weaknesses and strengths, supporting one another. You can find Stephenie's books and contact information at www.StephenieHovland.com.

BECKI JAMES is an ally to all who desire to live in God's presence. With an old friend flair, she gently guides hearts to God's throne. Whether ministering with pen or microphone, Becki's way with words nurtures Christ's love to all ages. She won two awards in the 2021 devotional *Wit, Whimsy, and Wisdom,* being honored for Best Overall Devotion and Best Women's Issues Devotion for her work titled, "Not Shaken." Find her at www.beckijames.com.

TERESA JANZEN, MEd, ignites a passion for abundant living through radical service. She is an international author, speaker, coach, and podcast host. More than twenty years of experience in global ministry drives her to share inspiring stories with wit and insight. Married to Dan, together they bridge cultures and continents serving primarily in sub-Saharan Africa and North America. Connect with Teresa at www.teresajanzen.com and tune in to the *Radical Abundance* podcast on your favorite platform.

Through her *Little Mama of Faith* blog, **TERRI KIRBY** delights audiences with her love of the Lord and a little laughter. Dwarfism, hospitalizations, international adoption, menopause, and a new season of singleness could have knocked her down to size but, instead, strengthened her faith. Never short on gratitude and humor, Terri encourages others in difficult seasons to rise as faith-filled giants. Author of several devotions, Terri is writing her first book. Visit her blog at www.littlemamaoffaith.com.

BETH KIRKPATRICK is a wife, mom, and grandmother who enjoys reading books and laughing with her friends. She strives to be a light for Jesus by being a good listener and sharing encouragement with others. After many years of working with elementary students, Beth now works with adults in a literacy ministry, Learning Matters! You can contact her at bethakirk@yahoo.com.

CARIN LeROY'S new book, *Where No Roads Go*, released this year and is available on Amazon. Her devotional stories tell of the adventures they experienced while church planting ministry in the remote jungle of Papua New Guinea. Carin is a piano teacher and works as an archivist. She has four adult children and six grandchildren. She lives in Orlando, Florida, with her husband, Dale.

LORI LIPSKY'S book, *Used Cookie Sheets*, brings forty-five of her very short stories together in a single collection. She's also a contributing author of the book *Wit, Whimsy & Wisdom*. Her character-driven stories point readers to a fresh perspective. Friend and family relationships are common themes in her work. Lori teaches piano at a private music school in Waunakee, Wisconsin. She and her husband, Mark, have two grown daughters and a granddaughter. www.lorilipsky.com

SANDY LIPSKY tries to sit still so she can compose the things God whispers in her ear. During the day, she writes and cares for her household. Nighttime finds her reading. Her first published article appeared in *Focus on the Family,* and her newest contributions may be found in the devotional book *Wit, Whimsy & Wisdom.* Sandy's motto is "Be a blessing." She enjoys Georgia weather and spending time with her husband and daughter. Visit Sandy at www.sandylipsky.com.

CHARLAINE MARTIN helps women discover God's great adventures in their everyday lives. Her work is published in *Wit, Whimsy & Wisdom* (A WordGirls collective devotional), guest blog posts, and several online publications. She is a fitness pro, seasoned speaker, and Christian wellness coach. Charlaine and her Boaz enjoy putzing around in their plane, cruising Florida bike trails, and sharing tickle bugs with their grandchildren. You can connect with her at www. charlainemartin.com.

DIANA LEAGH MATTHEWS has a heart for sharing God's love. Whether writing, singing, researching history, or working with seniors in nursing homes, she longs to shine for Christ. She is the author of *90 Breath Prayers for the Healthcare Professional, 90 Breath Prayers for the Caregiver*, the *90 Breath Prayer Journal*, and upcoming *90 Breath Prayers for those with Health Challenges*. Leagh shares hymn stories on her blog at www.DianaLeaghMatthews.com and hymn-votions on social media.

TLC NIELSEN works in a school library, sharing the love of stories with students and staff. In addition to being a Word Weaver writer, jazz trombonist, and gardener, TLC writes poetry and grants. She's editing her first fantasy novel, *By Land or Sea*. She contributed a tale or two in *I Believe in Healing* (Cecil Murphey and Twila Belk), *Stories of Grayslake* (Grayslake Historical Society), and most recently in *Wit, Whimsy & Wisdom* (a WordGirls collective).

Using her own family experiences to share the love of Jesus, **BETTY PREDMORE** enjoys encouraging women to pause and ponder the possibilities of life with Jesus. Betty has written two devotionals, *Pondering Virtue* and *Whispered Grace*. In addition, she has contributed to several collaborative devotionals, along with writing for numerous Christian magazines and blogs. Betty is a wife and mother of seven who enjoys spending time and making memories with her precious family.

JOANIE SHAWHAN shares true-life stories, offering her reader an eyewitness view of the action. Her Selah Awards finalist book, *In Her Shoes: Dancing in the Shadow of Cancer,* reflects the value of "Your story plus my story become our stories." An ovarian cancer survivor and registered nurse, Joanie speaks to medical students in the Survivors Teaching Students program. She co-founded an ovarian cancer social group: The Fried Eggs—Sunny-Side Up. Find Joanie at www.joanieshawhan.com

DOROTHY MAE SPRADLEY is an encourager, a pray-er, and a lay leader. She founded 2C1 Ministries to spread the care and comfort of Christ in ways that encourage us to see our one true Lord. She is currently working on a Bible study about waiting on the Lord. While Mae has taken a couple of seminary classes, most of her education comes from being a student of God's Word.

ROBIN STEINWEG finds life is "Sweet in the middle"—like the creamy center of a sandwich cookie! She's a contributing author of the book *Wit, Whimsy & Wisdom.* Find her writing at *The Christian Pulse, Keys for Kids, The Upper Room, Today's Christian Woman,* and *Music Teachers Helper* blog. Read her daily prayers for parents at "Prayerenting" on Facebook and encounter bits of positivity with songs on her YouTube channel. Access both at www.robinsteinweg.com.

GINA STINSON invites you to reclaim every day for God's glory. She's a pastor's wife and mom of two teenagers. Her first book, *Reclaimed: The Stories of Rescued Moments and Days*, released in 2020. She is featured in several anthologies and writes regularly for Lifeway's *Journey Magazine* for women. You can find Gina sharing the good news of Jesus, coupled with humor and hope, on social media or her website www.ginastinson.com.

VICKIE PRICE TAYLOR is a writer, teacher, and native West Virginian who loves hiking the trails of the beautiful Mountain State. She has published devotionals for *Penned From the Heart* and *Keys for Kids*. She is currently employed as a legal proofreader for a global law firm and has worked as a freelance editor for a number of fiction and nonfiction authors. Visit her blog at www.thissideofhope. wordpress.com and follow her on Instagram @vickiepricetaylor.

Intrigued and inspired by people and personalities, retired school counselor **HALLY WELLS** writes about faith, parenting, and mental illness. Hally's kid sampler pack includes biological, adopted, step, and foster. Each one, along with many students, has awed and exhausted her in beautiful ways. Hally helps overwhelmed parents find practical answers, impactful resources, faith-family support, and divine wisdom—digging deep enough to find the good stuff, reaching high enough to find the best! Visit Hally at www.hallyjwells.com.

God's Grin Gal, **KATHY CARLTON WILLIS**, writes and speaks with a balance of funny and faith, whimsy and wisdom. She coaches others to remove the training wheels of doubt and not just risk but also take pleasure in the joyride of life. Kathy's been dubbed as WordMama from the WordGirls. Check out her Grin & Grow Break video devotions on Facebook and her grinning Boston terrier logo in her Grin Gal book series. www.kathycarltonwillis.com

ANNIE WOLTER is a fun-filled Christian who loves to tell and write stories of God's faithfulness and of believers who have leaned on God to overcome big challenges. Having married for the first time at age 51, she especially relates to and shares about the issue of loneliness facing many single Christians. Discover her humorous and relatable writings at www.anniewolter.com. Look there for her book, *From Lonely to Loved*, in early 2022.

Inspired by illuminated manuscripts and stained-glass windows, **LISA-ANNE WOOLDRIDGE** helps others "Live life illuminated." She is often lost in wonder at the beauty of both Creator and creation as she's typing away. Her heartwarming stories have been published in several popular collections. *The Secret Circle*, her first cozy mystery, is now available online. You can find her at home—where the mountains meet the redwoods, and the redwoods meet the sea—or at www.Lisa-Anne.net.

Acknowledgments

This book was made possible due to some very special people. We want to acknowledge your support and help.

We have grateful gratitudes for:

Our buddy editors. Each devotion was edited by at least one buddy editor before the contributing author submitted the piece. Some devotions had input from multiple buddies. We couldn't have done this project without you. In addition to the contributing authors helping each other (a beautiful thing to watch!), we had the benefit of feedback from Sue Smith, Anita Klumpers, Shannon L. Landon, and Judyann Grant. Thank you for helping us out.

Our WordMama, Kathy Carlton Wills. You coordinated the project, mothered us to make improvements, and edited the complete book. Thank you for caring enough to make sure we give our best.

Our families and friends. You cheered us on and managed without us so we could write. You support our dreams and make us feel as if we're rock stars. This book is possible in part because of you.

Our editor and book designer, Michelle Rayburn. You made sure the book cover design and the interior design reflect our WordGirls brand as well as our hearts. The attention to detail you gave during our edits made sure we followed industry standards. We love the mid-century modern vibe. Thank you for our beautiful book!

Our churches. We value the fellowship of faith. Because of our heavenly Father, we are family.

Our Lord. May this book bring you all the glory. It is because of you and your Word that we have words. You bring our spiritual snapshots to life! We are pleased to be your WordGirls.

Our Debut Devotional

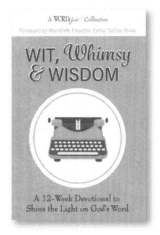

In addition to *Snapshots of Hope & Heart*, WordGirls has published *Wit, Whimsy & Wisdom*.

> "Our desire is for you to find nuggets within these
> pages that make you think, inspire you to worship, and
> even give you a few laughs along the way."

—Kathy Carlton Willis, founder of WordGirls

Seeking special time with God each day? *Wit, Whimsy & Wisdom* is here to be your guide. In each devotion, look for a concept you can refer back to in your thoughts as you go about your day. The stories will give you some grins, some grace, and some grit to help you through the struggles you face, as well as help you celebrate moments of victory.

This three-month devotional is divided into five relevant sections. Feel free to read it straight through or choose what you need that day. Our sections feature Worship & Prayer, Humor, Family, Spiritual Growth, and Women's Issues.

Wit, Whimsy & Wisdom was the first WordGirls devotional, designed to use God's Word and the words of WordGirls to help you fall in love even more with the Word made flesh—Jesus.

More 3G Books

Publisher Kathy Carlton Willis has a full line of books. Kathy's boldly practical tips, tools, and takeaways show up in Christian living books, Bible studies, and devo-studies. 3G Books are perfect for small groups or individual reading.

The Grin Gal's Guide to Wellbeing: Being Well in Body, Soul & Spirit

Being well begins from the inside out. This book is not just about Kathy's weight-loss and wellness journey. It's a guide for your pursuit of wellbeing. It doesn't provide a program for temporary behavior modification but a process for permanent God-led change.

On Kathy's quest for improved health, she discovered wellbeing is a balance of body, soul, and spirit. Her coaching style recognizes struggles, victories, aha! moments, and goals. She offers honesty, humor, and occasionally—homework!

The first section has chapters with the following features:

- Heartstrings (Stories)
- Heavenly Insights (Bible Study)
- Help Me! (Tools for Equipping)
- Homework (Making it Real)
- Health Check (Evaluation for Body/Soul/Spirit)
- Hurrahs and Happy Dances (Celebration of Victories)
- Hope Quest (Prayers)

The second section of the book includes practical resources. Join Kathy as a Wellbeing Warrior. Activate personal stewardship by creating your own care plan using the tools of this guide. You won't always see a cure, but you can have a better quality of life.

7 Trials Every Woman Faces: Is Job a Member of My Family Tree? (The Grin Gal's Guide to Trials)

Struggling with life challenges? You are not alone!

Ever wish for a friend who really understood you? *7 Trials Every Woman Faces* offers a virtual friend to lean on. Kathy comes alongside you as she shares insights learned through her own stinky situations.

All life trials fit in the same categories as Job's afflictions (told in the oldest book of the Bible). Whenever Kathy feels as if there's a "kick me" sign on her back, she asks, "Is Job a member of my family tree?" Laughing helps a little.

The chapter segments go along with the family tree theme:

- **Family Album.** Snapshots of heartwarming stories from real life.
- **Family Bible.** Biblical insights to overcome trials from a godly perspective.
- **Family Recipes.** Practical steps to help you grow and succeed God's way.
- **Family Legacy.** Lessons passed along as you help others endure trials.

Learn how to overcome Job-like trials when your family lets you down, friends misunderstand you, your health crumbles, your finances plummet, or others question your faith.

Everyone has trials, but it's the way we deal with hardship that determines not only the outcome but how we cope when we're smack-dab in the middle of them.

The Grin Gal's Guide to Joy: A Story, Study & Steps 7-Week Bible Study

If you've ever felt like the joy, joy, joy, joy down in your heart has gone missing, then this book is for you! Kathy learned that happiness runs and hides, but joy remains when trials show up. Now she's here to share these principles with you in *The Grin Gal's Guide to Joy*.

In each chapter:

- **Grin with Joy** tells real-life stories and observations. You'll laugh at Kathy's humorous confessions and wacky insights.
- **Grow with Joy** features a *joy* word study and workbook. Kathy explores what the Bible says and unpacks timely truths.
- **Go with Joy** offers life application. Pick the action steps that help you live a joy-filled life.
- **Give with Joy** equips you to share joy and meet the needs of others. This is when faith becomes ministry.
- Your **Grin with Joy Challenge** describes a joy-challenging scenario to solve.

The Ultimate Speaker's Guide: Practical Tips, Tools & Takeaways

The first book to kick off 3G Books was created with speakers in mind. Packed cover-to-cover with invaluable information, *The Ultimate Speaker's Guide* is the new bible for communicators.

With almost two decades of industry knowledge under her belt, Kathy Carlton Willis has coached hundreds of speakers to help them develop successful speaking businesses. This book covers all the tips, tools, and takeaways you'll need to ensure that your audience increases and your message is heard, including:

- Setting up your business
- Finding a brand that fits
- Getting more bookings
- Polishing your style
- Discovering God's plan for your business

An extensive resource section containing a sample contract, media interviewing tips, fee schedules, checklists, and much more, makes *The Ultimate Speaker's Guide* an essential toolkit you'll use time and again.

Made in the USA
Columbia, SC
30 October 2021